THE SPANISH DREAMER

A Biography of José Paronella

Dena Leighton

Edited by Lynne Hutton
Revised by Paronella Park 2007

THE SPANISH DREAMER

75 years at Paronella Park

2010 marks another exciting milestone for Paronella Park - 75 years since José Paronella first opened the doors to his Spanish Pleasure Garden in 1935.

The story told within this book, The Spanish Dreamer, contains many of the high points and low points from the early years at Paronella Park, leading up until José's death in 1948.

Since then, Paronella Park's unwritten story has continued.

When we arrived and discovered Paronella Park in 1993, it had suffered through a long period of neglect and decline. Gradually, we uncovered and re-discovered much of José's work, and, with the help of The Spanish Dreamer, began to share the remarkable story of José and his dream with our guests.

We could not have predicted the situation we find ourselves in now. Paronella Park has seen an enormous amount of success, won numerous Tourism Awards and been recognised as Queensland's number 1 attraction. All of this success has come as a result of the support of our visitors and has enabled us to continue on the work of the Paronellas and, to "keep the dream alive".

Over these years, we have not only had an opportunity to experience the wonders of José's project, and the opportunity to bring parts of it back to life (including the original Hydro Electric System that powered Paronella Park in the 1930's!), but also an opportunity to experience many of the trying natural wonders (floods and cyclones) that José faced as well. Most notable of these for us, was Cyclone Larry in March 2006.

We feel privileged and extremely fortunate to be involved in this incredible project. It's fair to say that we look on ourselves more as the custodians than as the owners of this remarkable place.

We are confident and excited about Paronella Park's future and would like to say a big thank you to all of our guests for their role in ensuring this important part of Australia's heritage is cared for as it should be.

The Dream Continues....

Mark & Judy Evans

© Copyright   M and J Evans 2007
Paronella Park
1733 Japoonvale Road
Mena Creek QLD 4871

All rights reserved. Except under the conditions described in the Copyright Act 1968 of Australia and subsequent amendments, no part of this publication may be reproduced, stored in a retrieval system, or transmitted in any form or by any means, electronic, mechanical, photocopying, recording or otherwise, without prior written permission of the copyright owners.

Dena Leighton has asserted her right to be identified as the author of this work.

First published by Rosemount Press in 1997
Published in 2007 by Paronella Park

National Library of Australia
Cataloguing-in-Publication data

Leighton, Dena.
The Spanish Dreamer: a biography of José Paronella.

ISBN 978-0-646-48494-5

Paronella, José, 1887-1948. 2. Spaniards – Queensland – Biography
Paronella Park (QLD.) – History. I. Title.

920.71

Printed in Australia by D&D Colour Printing, Virginia, Q.
Eleventh Printing December 2009

Photo Acknowledgements

Sincerest thanks for help with photo research
    Frank Gill
    Barbara and Derek Lamperd
    Adela Martin
    Elizabeth and Stanley Onaindia
    Paronella Family Members
    John Oxley Library
    Cairns and Innisfail Historical Societies

Prologue

It is early evening at Paronella Park. The sun has not yet set and casts long shadows across the paths. It is peaceful and quiet.

The last of the day's visitors have left, taking with them images of a Spanish Castle and Gardens; romantic visions and exotic beauty.

The ruins of José's dream blend back into the tropical vegetation. They, too, seem finally to be at peace. In a strange way, they are more beautiful now than when José built them. Green moss softens the concrete edges; the battlements and castellations have been rounded by weather and the passage of time.

If you stand very still and very quiet, you can hear the echo of sounds - children's laughter, the clink of teacups, a band tuning up and the gentle splashing of the fountain.

A small boy looks up at José.

"Do dreams really come true, Mr Paronella?"

This book is dedicated to

Teresa Zerlotti (1925 - 2008)
José Paronella's Daughter.

without whose help this book could not have been written

Teresa and Pino Zerlotti (October 2000)

Chapter One

In the North Eastern corner of Spain is the Province of Catalonia. It is a region of contrasts, where the terrain falls dramatically from the soaring heights of the Pyrenees to the jagged coastal cliffs of the Costa Brava. After heavy rain or when the snows melt, streams crash down the hillside. Yet in the lower valleys and foothills, there are endless rocky, arid stretches.

The summer weather is hot and dry; the winters can be extremely cold. In the late 19th century, few roads led into this remote countryside. There were only rough dirt tracks, dusty in summer, muddy and rutted in winter. Leaving the road from Llanca to El Port de las Selva, a narrow track led steeply uphill. Bordered on one side by a roughly built stone wall, it was passable only on foot or by mule.

Eventually, it struggled round a last curve to reach a group of cottages clinging to the side of the hill- the small village of La Vall de Santa Creu.

Here, José Pedro Enrique Paronella was born, on 26th February 1887. Most of the homes were only crudely built mud huts, just a basic shelter from the elements. The Paronella cottage was a little more substantial. Built of stone and mud, it has a white stucco exterior and a red tiled roof. There were two rooms, one for eating and living; the other for sleeping. Under the house was a storage area and the kitchen was a separate building at the rear. A stone wall divided the Paronella casa from it's neighbours, with entry from the lane through a green wooden gate set in the stonework.

Pedro and Maria Paronella reared six children, the youngest of whom was José.

Life was hard for everyone. The men worked long hours in the hot sun, tending the olives, which grew so profusely in the dry summers. Pedro always dreamed of having his own farm but this was never to be. He worked in the olive fields for a local farmer.

The women also helped with the olives but their prime responsibility was the home, including the vegetable garden, the fowl and probably a goat or two. It was a peasant existence- simple but demanding.

There was no electricity. Oil lamps and candles were used after dark, though only for a few hours. It was an early to bed, up at dawn lifestyle.

Water was not laid on to the cottages. A crystal clear stream ran down from the mountain and was channelled to a spout for drinking water and a communal pool for washing clothes.

For José's mother Maria, there was much heavy, tiring work- carrying water, hand washing all the family's clothes, cooking meals, gardening in the rocky soil. And watching over her six children.

Yet there was strong family support and a sense of loyalty. All the generations of the Paronella family pulled together, to make even this basic living. Grandparents were valued for their advice, and to look after the younger children while Maria helped Pedro in the fields.

Maria's mother, Eleanor, was a familiar figure to José. She was very severe-looking, dressed all in black, with her grey hair pulled into a tight bun at the back of her head.

Occasionally, in the evenings, she would unbend and take José onto her knee. The elder children would gather round to hear Grandma's wonderful stories of romantic Spanish castles and the 'nobleza' whose lives were filled with drama and excitement. José loved these tales. They made a deep impression on him.

Maria prepared simple but substantial and tasty meals for her family. Ingredients came from the local area- chickens and the occasional rabbit, cheese, dried mushrooms, olive oil, honey, flour, and nuts. To these she added produce from her own garden - eggs, vegetables, especially tomatoes and peppers, and herbs such as oregano, rosemary, thyme, and bay leaves.

D. JOSE LLOVERAS RICART   Presbítero, Cura PARROCO de EL PORT DE LA SELVA, Obispado de Gerona, Provincia de GIRONA

CERTIFICO: Que en el libro de bautismos número 12 folio 151, que se guarda en el archivo de esta Parroquia de mi cargo, hay inscrita una partida que copiada a la letra dice así: " a los diecinueve de marzo de mil ochocientos ochenta y siete, yo el infrascrito cura-párroco de la iglesia parroquial de San Esteban de Mata de la villa de la Selva de Mar, Obispado de Gerona, bauticé en la pila bautismal de la misma a José Pedro, Enrique, nacido a los veinte y seis del próximo pasado febrero, hijo legítimo de Pedro Paronella y Maria de los Dolores Buxeda, naturales y vecinos de La Vall, sufragánea de esta parroquia. Abuelos paternos: Jaime, natural de La Vall y Maria Amaliach de Rosas, consortes. Abuelos maternos: Pedro, natural de La Vall y Eleonor Font de Padret y Marsá. Padrinos: José Massó, natural de Vilamaniscle y Enrica Paronella de La Vall, hermana del bautizado.-Baudilio Pujol, cura-parróco. rubricado.-

NOTA MARGINAL: a los 16 de septiembre de 1925, contrajo matrimonio en La Vall con Margarita Soler Roig. Testigos: Pedro Roig Esteban Peronella. Doy fe. Pedro Povesa. pbro.

Concuerda en todo con el original al que me refiero, y para que conste a los efectos oportunos libro el presente, sellado con el de la Parroquia en El Port de La SELVA nueve de octubre de mil novecientos noventa y cinco.

Firma

Copy of José's Baptismal Certificate

On special occasions, Maria would make her own sausages; Buttifarra, a white cooked sausage and Fuet, similar to Salami.

The villagers supported each other, especially in times of trouble. José remembered one of the men, Pedro Soler, who lived nearby. He kept bees and would exchange honey for vegetables from Maria's garden. One day something went terribly wrong and the bees attacked him.

He was stung all over his legs and arms and neck. He died the next day.

He left a wife and six children, 3 boys and 3 girls. All the neighbours helped. They looked after the young ones, brought gifts of food and above all, shared the family's grief with genuine and ongoing support.

Two of the Soler girls were to figure in José's life in later years.

Tragedy came soon after to the Paronella family. Maria was pregnant again but died during a miscarriage. One of the older girls took over, caring for the family.

Few of the adult villagers could read or write. José, with the other children, went to school - but it was a long hot walk of several kilometres and any excuse was a reason for being absent.

"Dad needed me in the fields."

"I had to help Mum pluck some fowl."

José left school early to look for work. There were no jobs to be found in the local area, so he moved away to a small town, where one of his married brothers lived.

He was fortunate to find a good job in a bakery. The work was hard and the hours long, but he was learning a trade.

Living with his relations, however, was to prove difficult. José's brother and his wife had only a very small house, and there really wasn't room for him. And the wife resented him being there and made him feel very unwelcome.

José stuck it out for a couple of years while he learnt the bakery trade but he was unhappy and restless. One day, after a particularly bad row, he made an eventful decision. He would move away on his own. Somehow he would cope. He had heard about the Navarra Province. One of the regular customers at the bakery had told him of it's beauty.

"Soaring peaks, deep luxuriant valleys, swift-flowing rivers and tranquil pastureland. And then there is Pamplona. You must see Pamplona. Lots of shops and cafes. Plenty of work - especially for a good baker."

José told his relatives he was leaving. First he would go back to La Valle to see family and friends and then to Pamplona.

Back in La Valle, an important meeting took place, between José's father, Pedro and the widow Soler. The elder Soler daughter, Matilda, was unmarried. A tall dark haired and very beautiful girl, she was a year or so younger than José.

The families agreed that she would be betrothed to José. The arrangement was confirmed with a handshake - in Catalan culture this was a more binding agreement than any legal documentation. The honour of both families was involved.

José left la Valle in June and arrived in Pamplona in the midst of the town's preparations for the Fiesta de San Fermin. It was a good time to be there, with plenty of workers needed to help cater for the hundreds of visitors. He soon found work and cheap lodgings and before long began to really enjoy the vivacity and excitement of life in a vibrant, colourful city.

Physically, he was now a very attractive young man. He was slim and athletic-looking, with dark wavy hair and mischievous brown eyes. He was popular with the girls and temporarily forgetting his arrangement with Matilda, he had a great social life.

Years later he talked with nostalgic affection of his time in Pamplona. It was certainly a long way from La Valle in every sense.

However, more changes were in the wind.

Sitting one day drinking coffee at an outdoor café, José was reading the newspaper. An advertisement caught his eye.

'Workers wanted in Australia to labour on railway construction.'

Though he never answered the advert, it turned his mind towards emigration. He knew of family friends who had already taken the plunge and were making new lives for themselves. Their letters home told of enormous opportunities for work, and the good money they were making. Some even sent money home to their families to pay for passage for brothers and sisters.

What did José have to lose? He had enough money for his fare and a bit over. He was 25 years old, fit and free.

Except - there was his agreement with Matilda.

He did not want to take her with him to an unknown situation. She would want to settle down in one area. He might want to move around he argued to himself: 'It would be better to go ahead on my own and send for her when I have made some money.'

Whilst José was trying to make up his mind, events in European politics helped his decision. There were rumblings of war. If he did not leave soon, hostilities might break out and prevent his departure.

He sent a message to Matilda, withdrew all his savings and booked a passage to Australia. The ship was the Seydlitz, a twin screw steamer which plied the Far Eastern and Australia routes. She sailed from Bremen and José boarded in Genoa.

The voyage was uneventful and José arrived in Sydney on 24th July 1913. He was 26 years old.

José Stayed in the city only long enough to have a look around. Compared to Pamplona, Sydney seemed open and spacious, with wide roads, huge parks and many empty spaces.

He went on a ferry across the harbour. It was an unusual day for Sydney, with a wintry chill and gray skies threatening rain.

He cut his planned stay short and boarded one of the numerous coastal steamers which covered the route up to Queensland.

José's original idea was to seek work in the North Queensland canefields, around Innisfail. On the voyage from Europe, so many Spanish and Italian men were planning to head up there - to form canecutting gangs.

But one of the passengers had told him of other work, in the mining industry around the Cloncurry Region.

"That's the place to make a fortune! Thousands have retired millionaires!"

José decided to try mining first. He arrived in August 1913.

Queensland's North West was a remote, sparsely populated area. Close to the Northern territory border, it was 1854 kilometres from Brisbane.

They countryside which greeted José was bone dry, with little vegetation apart from twisted shrubs and Spinifex.

The land is mainly flat, except for the ancient granite hills, known as the Selwyn Ranges. These intrusions on the flat landscape are more than 600 million years old and are the remains of once huge mountains.

This region first came to notice in the last 1860's, when the discovery of gold first sparked a rush. Selwyn's population exploded and it developed into a typical mining camp, with hard-living, hard-drinking prospectors and the usual hangers-on.

At almost the same time, copper was discovered and places like nearby Cloncurry began to flourish. It became the centre of a very rich mining field. Four smelters were working and there was plenty of work.

But it was hard labour. And it was made worse by the climate. Cloncurry holds a weather record never topped anywhere else in Australia. On 16 July 1889, the temperature reached 51 degrees in the shade!

In 1913, when José came, the demand for copper was increasing. War was imminent and the mineral was needed, amongst other things, for shell casings.

Though glad to find well-paid work so quickly, José was appalled at the conditions. Selwyn was a shanty town, a dump of a place, with a few ramshackle buildings. Families lived in shacks. The single workers had only tents, often filthy and torn, with no ground sheets against vermin and snakes.

José could only stand it for four months. He needed to return to the more acceptable climate of the coast and hopefully, to better working conditions.

He arrived in the South Johnstone area just after New Year 1914. The cane season was coming to an end. He was able though, to find odd jobs on the farms. And he took time to look around this countryside. It was totally alien to anything he had ever experienced before.

He was now in the tropical wet belt, known as the green heart of the North.

José could not believe there could be so much rain in the whole world. It felt like sheet upon sheet of water.

A foot of rain in a single day was here hardly newsworthy! And José arrived in one of their wettest years.

The Seydlitz, the ship on which José travelled to Australia

    But the vegetation nourished by the rain, the lush rich tropical growth, fascinated José. After the glary whiteness of the Selwyn landscape, his eyes relished the range of greens and golds, the native bush interspersed with the square patches of cultivated cane. The soil was the colour of ploughed chocolate, and dark red tracks led to farm gardens with bougainvillea vines and ripe mangoes and pawpaws.

    From those very first months, José felt at home in this tropical region. He began to hope and to dream. He felt optimistic.

    And the locals assured him that, as soon as the slack was over, he would find a place in a canecutting gang.

Edith Street - Innisfail

Chapter Two

It was the start of the canecutting season that José hated the most.

The pain from his hands was almost unbearable. His skin bubbled with dozens of blisters, raw and red. He tried rubbing meths in but it didn't help.

The old timers suggested urine.

"Piss on a strip of cloth and wrap it around your hand."

Even this brought no relief. José knew the only cure was more agony, until the friction of caneknife against hand made blisters go deeper and deeper and eventually turn into rock hard callouses.

He had seen a fight onces between two Italians outside the hotel. One was big and strong, with huge fists; but he was no match for his slighter opponent - a canecutter, who used not his fists, but the palm of his hand, hard as a block of solid steel.

José and his team finished in the field at 6.00pm that first evening. The idea of a shower felt great, until the cold water hit raw skin and aching muscles. Every part of his body was in pain. Back and legs ached, shoulders ached, even his finger joints ached.

He ate his meal without tasting it and sat down on the verandah of the barracks, in a blur of weariness. Soon it was 10.00pm and well past the time for bed. He had to be up before dawn, ready for another day's work.

José tried to stand up, but all his joints had stiffened. He had to painfully unwind his muscles, one by one. He could hear protesting cracks. He was shaking like a leaf, just with the effort of getting to his feet.

The night was even worse. His body relived the agony of the day - twitching and thrashing. He dozed off but nightmares woke him. He tried to move into a comfortable position but his limbs were screaming. He could hear his room mate groaning in the other bunk.

When finally he fell into a fitful sleep, he was awakened by possums sliding down the sloping tin roof.

It would be weeks before José's body adjusted and hardened to the labour.

Sometimes, in the paddocks, José allowed himself to think of home. The hot, dry summers and cool winters.

Nothing could be further from this place; the sauna conditions under a tropical sun, bent down fighting the cane, the heat, the humidity and the sweat running even from your eyes.

The tall cane gave little shade and stopped any cooling breeze with it's dense growth.

He drank gallons of water, never even feeling it go down - and it came straight out his pores. Some of José's gang were already suffering from prickly heat. His own skin was beginning to chafe under his belt.

He told himself to get with the rhythm - hold it, cut it, put it on the pile.

An old hand, a fellow Spaniard, had told him to keep to the pattern - "Grasp 2-3 stalks chest high, level with your heart; with razor sharp knife, slash with one smooth movement, just above ground level. Then throw the stalks forward in line ready for gathering into bundles."

José was glad that this year he was working in a good team, with men he knew - six from Spain and two Italians. His first season had been bad. José had only just arrived and helped make up a scratch team. Not used to the hard work, he had worried that he wouldn't be able to keep pace. One of the Australians had called him a 'weed'. He'd had to ask what it meant?

"You're not pulling your weight!"

José thought at first that his physique was against him. Later he realised that his wiry, sinewy thinness was actually an advantage.

José (back row, 4th from right) enjoying smoko with local farmers and canecutters

And he had learned the imperative of a sharp knife. The iron filing stick stood in the paddock. José worked his knife until it would cut through the cane without resistance. He also experimented by shortening the handle and adjusting the blade to a better cutting angle.

Work started at dawn, when the men arrived in the paddocks dressed for the day's work. It was almost a uniform that they wore - long pants or shorts, a flannel shirt or singlet, broad-brimmed hat and a towel strip around the neck.

José preferred long trousers as they gave better protection against Hairy Mary, the prickles which cover the cane. You couldn't see the prickles but you could surely feel their irritation, as they worked their way into your skin, causing painful rashes.

The day began with the worst part of the canecutter's job - loading the wagons. This took 2-3 hours, depending on the size of the rake going in. Morning dew covered everything.

The work was done on the run. The cut was on contract and time meant money. José knew from last season that it was no good busting a gut lifting big bundles. Speed was the only way to go.

When the wagons were loaded, everyone was ready for morning Smoko. Some days it would be drizzling but the gang sank thankfully to the ground, drenched in rain and dew and sweat. José ate his sandwiches quickly, before they too became sodden.

Then the cutting of the cane began, and, with a stop over lunchtime, went on till mid afternoon. After another Smoko, it was time to move the rails for the next day's loading. At times, they would be red hot and José had learned to lift them with a bunch of leaves to protect his hands.

As the season went on, there would be other problems. Bees and March flies loved the sugary smell of the broken cane. José had seen cutters working with swollen, bee-stung hands.

Accidents were frequent. One of José's gang hit a vine with his knife. The razor sharp edge flew back at him, slicing deeply into his thigh.

And then there was Leptospirosis, commonly known as Weil's disease. The Leptospirae were present in rat's urine - and rats in their thousands lived in the trash. The fevers were often fatal. There didn't seem to be much the doctors could do.

José's birthplace - La Vall de Santa Creu

The Paronella cottage where José spent his childhood

José crossed himself that he had so far escaped these additional agonies.

But he wondered how much longer his luck would hold out. He felt a tremendous urge to move away from canecutting.

There was plenty of time to think whilst working in the cane paddocks. Perhaps the regular rhythm suited the mind's musings?

Many of his friends spent the time thinking of the past, of their family and homes far away at the other end of the world. Their homesickness and loneliness grew, fuelled by the alien environment, the foreign language and the primitive living conditions.

For José, it was different. He thought mostly of the future and the day when he would own his own farm. He would employ teams of canecutters and would never himself have to cut cane!

Occasionally, he thought of Matilda. He would write to her one day soon.

The next season, José had a stroke of good luck. He was in town one day near the end of the slack season and was introduced to the leader of one of the gangs.

"Heard you used to be a baker back in Spain. We need a cook for our gang. Want to join us?"

José was about to say that being a baker didn't mean he could cook, at least not in the way needed for the ravenous appetites of a cane cutting team. Then he thought:

"No more cutting cane! No more aching limbs and endless slog in the field."

And he would still get his equal share of the cutting money. "Sure, I can cook. I join you."

Though José still had to help at times with setting the rails, his main job would be to prepare meals for his gang, cut wood for the stove, carry water - and look after the barracks.

Their barracks that year were isolated and primitive. The long building was set off the ground on low stumps. A verandah ran right along the front, reached by 4-5 wooden steps.

The structure was covered in corrugated iron - walls and roof. There were no internal linings. In place of windows, the men propped up hinged sheets of corrugated iron, which let in light, air and the inevitable wild life. The worst were the huge moths attracted by the light from the kerosene lamps. It was a dilemma whether to swat them or suffer them - for when flattened with a good aim from a rolled up newspaper, they paid you back by the awful smell from their dying bodies.

From the verandah, 6 doors led to the bedrooms, each for 2 men. Again, basics only. A bunk on each side - maybe a packing case for a table. A kerosene lamp hung from the ceiling.

The kitchen where José worked was separate at the end of the building, with its smokestack the only brick part of the barracks. Inside was a basic wood stove, an old door set on tressles to act as a table and an air-cooled safe for perishables suspended on chains from the ceiling. Utensils were basic. There was no running water.

From this primitive kitchen, José soon learned to prepare three huge meals a day, plus lunch, afternoon tea and even supper!

The men needed to replenish the enormous amounts of energy they expended. They demanded large quantities of nutritious food. Steak was eaten for all meals, and bacon, chickens, eggs, cornbeef hash, bread and local fruits - pawpaws, pineapples, mangoes, bananas.

To this traditional Aussie fare, José added some European touches, with pasta and rice and occasional herbs, to improve the flavour.

On the verandah of the barracks was a shower recess, with only cold water, coming from a rainwater tank on the side of the building. At least in this climate, they never ran out of water! There was also a set of laundry tubs, where the men washed their own clothes, usually on a Saturday morning.

Toilets were away from the building, in a small outhouse, a pit type earth closet.

Newcomers were always shocked at their first sight of the accommodation. It seemed to them little better than housing for animals!

The farmers resented spending time and money on maintaining the barracks. It was often left to the men to do repairs or make improvements.

Nature didn't help. Ants invaded the kitchen; mould grew on everything; and the rats were impossible to control. Poison was no good. Dead rats were simply replaced with new ones coming out of the cane.

At night, nature did its best to make sure the men didn't sleep, with the husky cough of possums and the wailing of night birds - and the inevitable mosquitoes.

Yet the men came back, year after year.

Some say it was the money; others say they came for the mateship, to be part of a team; some certainly came for the social life.

At weekends, Innisfail came to life as a noisy, rollicking place to have a good time. The cutters had two free days and made the most of them. Some drank themselves stupid and had to be thrown into the back of a ute on Sunday afternoon and driven back to the farm. Others spent their money gambling, with large groups gathered in the hotel, waiting for race reports from Brisbane. And then there were the brothels. Every need was catered for.

José was different. He didn't spend his money on booze and he didn't gamble.

But he was handsome and virile and an excellent dancer. He was much in demand at dances and social functions. Many a Spanish mother must have had an eye on him, for an arranged marriage for her daughter. However, José played the field, with lots of girlfriends, but no special sweetheart.

"Matilda is waiting for me in Spain, when I have made my fortune," José reminded himself.

Over meals at the barracks, talk often turned to the possibility of a cutter buying his own farm. José always listened carefully to such conversations. He held on to his dream of becoming a landowner. He knew it was possible. He had seen other men achieve it, especially fellow Spaniards and some Italians.

These men from Southern Europe were highly ambitious. They could see the opportunities which Australia offered and were determined to acquire their own farms.

Many had come, as José himself, from large families who barely scratched an existence from small plots of land. For younger sons, especially, there was the need to move away, to make a future for themselves.

Pioneer canefarmers from No.1 Branch, South Johnstone. Note the snakes!

In their thousands, they had come to Australia, determined to make good.

Their background gave them undoubted advantages. They were used to working on the land, and the long hard hours of labour. They were used to high temperatures and soon acclimatised to Queensland conditions.

Though the Southern European cane gangs were accepted by the farmers as cheap, reliable labour, there was also a sense of suspicion and distrust. Their attitudes seemed 'Un-Australian'; the intensity of their desire for land was incomprehensible to Australians, used to ownership of land as a natural way of life. Their degree of hard work and the incredible group support system which existed amongst them - these were not normal! They represented a very real 'take-over' threat.

Yet it was mainly Irish held farms, which passed into Southern European hands. The Irish, raised in a cold Northern climate, did not adapt easily to tropical conditions. They were also particularly prone to tuberculosis, for which there was no known cure.

With the Irish love of company and drinking, the many pubs and grog-selling shanties proved irresistible. They became their haven from the humid heat. Unfortunately, their farms suffered and many, heavily mortgaged, were taken back by the banks and resold. Inevitably, the new landowner was an Italian or Spanish migrant.

José was a Southern European and held all their beliefs and attitudes regarding land. But he also possessed an extra quality - a clear business mind.

He knew which farms were coming on the market cheaply, because they were rundown. There was talk of such things at the barracks. And they spoke of the enormous profits being made.

"Did you hear about Prosper Covacevich? He's bought a farm at South Johnstone for £4000. He reckons he'll sell it for double that in 3-4 years time!"

José also knew about land available from the government. Provided it was cleared, planted to cane and developed, it could be resold at great profit.

Back on his bunk, José stretched out, his hands behind his head.

'Soon, very soon, they will be talking about me and the land I bought. I will become a farmer, an owner of land.'

An amazing sight - cane fires.

Mena Creek Falls from José's Picnic Area

The Bridge and Stairs leading to the Bamboo Forest and Teresa Falls

José's Picnic Tables

José's Cottage and Gardens

Chapter Three

José stood looking at the stretch of rainforest.

Timber getters had been through it in the last century, taking out the valuable silky oaks, cedars, black bean and kauri pines.

But now the tropical jungle vegetation had closed over and left no trace of their passage. The scrub was almost impenetrable.

This was the first land which José purchased. He planned to clear it and establish a cane farm. He could not afford to buy an established property. Besides, he hoped to make a large profit when he eventually sold - and he could best do this by starting from scratch.

But his heart fell when he stood ready to begin the mammoth task.

The strong vines and creepers had to be attacked first. But it was truer to say that it was the jungle which attacked any man foolhardy enough to come near.

Hooked vines locked the trees together. Lawyer vines, known locally as 'Wait-a-Whiles', grabbed your clothes, your hair, your skin. They could not be pulled straight out. You had to back off (hence the name) and pull the thorns out from the direction they had grasped you.

One old timber-getter told José:

"Just touch them and they grab you as though they are alive. They can stop running cattle in their tracks"

The strength of the lawyer vine was indeed legendary. It was said that, in the last century, a bushman was sitting relaxing in his camp. He was lassoed by an Aborigine, who was hiding in an overhanging tree. The noose was made of lawyer vines. The bushman was dragged away, killed and eaten.

Local school-children also recall its whippy power. Teachers were fond of cutting thick pieces of the vine, to punish 'errant ways'.

Nowhere else on earth was there a heavier growth of vines amongst large trees. It seemed as though the tropical vegetation was joined in hostile and barbarous war against any invader.

The only way in was to slash through with a machete, then use a brush hook and axe or handsaw, to cut out the saplings and thinner trees.

It was not only hard work, done in appalling conditions - it was also very dangerous. Trees or branches did not always fall as José intended. Sometimes they broke suddenly at a weak joint and fell without warning; or they tangled in vines and then, as their weight freed them, fell unexpectedly and often, dangerously close.

Then the largest trees had to be felled. José borrowed draught-horses to help drag the trunks away.

And still the jungle did not give in.

The stumps proved very hard to remove. They would be burnt and then left to rot. It would be five or six years before some stumps and roots rotted away. The silky oaks, in particular, were notorious for their refusal to give up. Eventually, José dynamited them out of the ground.

When enough land was finally cleared, José began to cultivate the soil. But with stumps and roots still in his way, he had to do all the work manually with a hoe.

Then he made mattock holes in which to plant the young cane.

The only advantage from all this hard work was that he did not need fertiliser. The combination of ash and virgin soil ensured good soil condition. And the climate helped, with high rainfall, spread throughout the growing season.

When José had harvested his first crop, he breathed a sigh of deep satisfaction.

'Now I am truly a canefarmer'.

With this status came a new respect from friends and from the other local farmers. And a lot more responsibility.

Whilst working as a cutter, José had learnt a great deal about the crop and the major problems with growing and harvesting the cane. Seeing this at second hand, however, was vastly different from making his own decisions, hiring workers and paying bills.

It was a fast learning curve. He needed to cultivate his land and consider the various strains of cane he would grow. The South Johnstone farmers were a supportive group and advice was freely given to the newcomer.

"Come over to my place and I'll show you how this new strain of cane handles so much better."

Sugarcane cultivation was not without its share of pests - the most damaging being the cane beetle. The larvae munched their way through the fields. They hatched in the summer months. As well as taking nutrients from the soil, the beetles also fed on the cane roots.

Whole crops were being devastated. Some areas were worse hit than others.

It was thought that the beetles bred in trees, so the Basilisk Range was cleared as a defensive measure. It seemed, however, to make no real difference. Other steps had to be taken or the cane industry would be wiped out altogether.

One method which appealed to the children of the district was Beetle Drives. At Christmas time, millions of beetles emerged from the ground and flew all over the area. They settled in trees.

The Cane Board offered to buy the beetles by the gallon!

Everyone went 'beetling'.

Years later, local resident Mena Fallon recalled her childhood summers and the wonderful pocket money they earned.

"Mum woke us up at 3.30am and we set off. We took a bed sheet with us and spread it under a likely tree. Then we climbed into the tree and shook every branch violently. Hundreds of beetles would drop onto the sheet. The problem was, they could crawl pretty quickly, so we had to slide down and collect them in our syrup tins, before they could bore into the ground."

Mena added "Grey backs were the best - the largest. We filled our tins faster!"

Individual farmers, scornful of the partial success of 'beetling', often came up with their own attempts at a solution.

The Ibis was found to be a good scavenger and one Italian farmer had a tame flock, which would follow him as he ploughed.

The most ingenious was a method used by Chinese farmers. They planted a mothball under each stook of cane. One of the earliest attempts at the chemical control of pests!

Besides the beetles, José also had to deal with bad weather, when storms damaged the cane, laying it flat. In these circumstances, the cutters were able to negotiate higher rates to compensate for the difficult conditions, which slowed down their rate of cutting.

It had been different when José was himself working in a cane gang.

José, at age 34, now a wealthy man

Then, he had benefited from the extra pay. Now, he was the one who had to pay out.

Despite the hard work and problems, José was relating to the tropical countryside of his adopted home. Sometimes he would go outside at night. The atmosphere was heavy, the air steaming. He could almost feel nature pulsing. He hoped for a cooling storm. Looking across the lush, moisture charged foliage of his paddocks, he saw the promise of another good crop.

José was steadily beginning to make money from his farm - so much so that he soon sold it for a profit.

In the next few years, he bought, improved and resold about twelve canefarming properties. Steadily he was amassing a considerable amount of money.

José now began to look for other ways to invest his fortune. He looked inland, towards the mining areas.

The terrain climbed sharply from the coastal strip and reached the plateau of the Atherton and Evelyn Tablelands. These areas had been created by huge volcanic eruptions.

The countryside was green and fertile - the climate temperate.

As you travelled west, however, the landscape changed. Lush greens gave way to dry, rough country on the edge of the spinifex. This region, covering the settlements of Herberton, Irvinebank, Ravenshoe and Mount Garnet, was the centre of the mineral belt.

Prospectors in the last century had found tin, copper, lead and zinc in this contact belt of granite and sandstone.

Some of the tin was alluvial, such as the enormous quantities found in the Gregory and Emu Creeks. The miners built up the boulders into walls to facilitate the workings. The floor was a series of burrows and open tunnels.

But the majority of the minerals were won from open-cut or underground mines.

Herberton became the centre for a lucrative tin field. In 1880, Willie Jack and John Newell had found the lode which became the Great Northern. In 1881, eighty bullocks were used to haul up the complete battery for the mine.

Nearby, Irvinebank was developing as a thriving community, with its School of Arts and branch of the National Bank.

Mount Garnet was basing its wealth on copper, alluvial tin and open cut tin mines. The local hotel displays, amongst other items from these boom days, a set of false teeth made from tin!

It was to these areas that José looked for another way to invest and to increase his fortune. He had already become familiar with the mining scene on his brief stay at Mount Selwyn, when he first came to Australia.

But this time, he would be the owner of a mine, not the labourer. He purchased a tin mining lease and work began. The mine was open-cut, just holes in the ground, cave-like, following the reef. The tin was easily won.

And the prices were reasonable.

José worked there himself, as well as employing labourers, including some aboriginals.

The days were long, starting at dawn. The men would not return to their camp until after dark. Food was basic, and consisted mainly of corned beef and damper.

José loved this country, with its rarefied atmosphere and the breezes which came up in the early afternoon.

He found the landscape peaceful; and was fascinated by the range of bird life - magpies, parrots, butcher-birds; wattle-birds squabbling in the trees; a flock of white cockatoos floating across the gorge and the call of a crow echoing sadly from the other side.

But all too soon, José's farming activities would draw him back to the coast.

He had also developed another business interest - money lending. In this era, though some men borrowed from the banks, there were many other, less structured loans available. Some of these were negotiated through solicitors. If a man had spare cash, he could pay it into his solicitor's Trust Fund and then it could be loaned out, with profit coming to both solicitor and lender.

José used an even less formal arrangement.

When he had cash available and was not yet ready to invest it in another farm of his own, he would loan the money to fellow Spaniards or to Italian friends. It was all done on a handshake, with no formal written agreements. There was never any shortage of borrowers, with so many men wanting to set themselves up on their own farms.

By making his money work for him in this way, José added considerably to his fast growing fortune.

For some time now, a dream had been developing in José's mind. He had never forgotten the beautiful castles which his grandmother had described. Whilst working in Pamplona, he had visited several. He imagined building such a Spanish style castillo, here in tropical Australia. He would set it in lush gardens and open it to visitors, as a tourist attraction.

Up to this point, José had lived and worked in Australia as an 'alien'. He had been issued with his Aliens Registration Certificate Number 105 at South Johnstone.

In 1921, José decided to confirm his intention to stay in Australia, as a resident and businessman, by applying for naturalisation.

The inscription later to be used on the Canecutter's Monument in Innisfail, echoed José's own belief.

'Ubi bene, ibi patria'.

'Where it goes well with me, there is my fatherland'.

José employed the firm of Normal R Mighell, Solicitors, to do the paperwork for his naturalisation.

On 20th August, he officially renounced his allegiance to the King of Spain and on 5th October 1921 José Paronella became an Australian citizen.

He was now 34 years old - and a very wealthy man.

Copy of José's Certificate of Naturalisation, 1921

Chapter Four

One day, José returned from a trip to town. An unmarked letter had been pushed under his door. He opened it - to find an extortion note, threatening dire consequences if he did not hand over £500 in cash.

It was signed, ironically,

Thanking you in anticipation,

Your friends,

The Black Hand.

At the bottom was a black ink impression of a human hand.

José's feelings were in turmoil. There was a terrible anger, and underneath, a cold fear.

No one, but no one took a Black Hand threat lightly.

Yet, José knew already, that he would not pay up.

'I worked very, very hard for my money. Never will I give it to these crooks.'

Such an attitude might be considered brave, moral, strong, but it could also be seen as foolhardy, considering the reputation of these shadowy extortion gangs.

The Black Hand movement was just surfacing in North Queensland in the 1920's. It was an 'accredited' branch of the Camorra of Italy and the Mafia of Sicily. The criminal organisation made its money from the profits of prostitution and the White Slave traffic and from blackmail and extortion.

It already had strong footholds in Melbourne and Sydney. It was inevitable that it would spread to the lucrative areas of the North Queensland cane country.

The Innisfail region had the largest and wealthiest colony of Italians in Australia. Land and farm prices were booming; there were high earnings and an abundance of cash.

The Black Hand's target would be the hundreds of well-to-do Italian farmers and the thousands of cash rich canecutters.

If threats were to be effective, the Black Hand had to follow up with severe reprisals against those who ignored their demands.

In a period of ten years, there were, in the Innisfail district, 11 murders, 30 bombings and 100's of blackmail and extortion letters handed to the police - and thousands which never surfaced.

All the efforts of the police were of no avail. A wall of silence was set up around Black Hand crime. Witnesses refused to testify - not surprising, when we know that the movement intimidated even judges and juries. They were to go as far as geligniting the Crown Prosecutor's home on the eve of a Black Hand trial.

The criminals openly scorned the police and their efforts to catch and convict. They were safe in the knowledge that, when a man's life and that of his loved one's were threatened, he soon 'forgot' what he had seen. They built their success on fear.

And then there was the evidence to demonstrate to those who ignored their notes, just what 'dire consequences' entailed. Retribution came in the form of houses and shops bombed; cane fields set on fire; animals killed and even the murder of one's wife and children.

Many Italians took their own precautions. They set up high fences around their homes to prevent bombs being thrown in; they kept noisy watchdogs; they installed bells and alarms.

José must have known for some time that they would turn their attention to him. After all, he qualified as a prime target. He was a prosperous man, who did his business in cash.

Though their usual victims were Italian, they were not averse to pressing any nationality for money, especially if they had blackmail threats to hold over them.

And this they did with José.

Not only was José totally opposed to paying money to the Black Hand, he was also reluctant to pay taxes to the government.

In his native Catalonia, personal income tax was not part of the revenue system. José didn't see why it should be any different in Australia.

'I earned this money. I keep this money!'

Eventually, however, he had been forced to put in tax returns and there was a large amount of tax outstanding, even though José's books vastly understated his profits and dealings.

He suspected that the Black Hand members knew of this.

Fortunately, like many of his friends, José kept a shotgun handy at his house.

Late one evening, he was in the kitchen. Alerted by the dog's cocked ears, José crept to the window. Someone was working their way across to the house.

José didn't hesitate.

He thrust his gun through the glass, fired two shots and yelled:

'If you ever come back here, I'll kill you!'

Brave or foolhardy, we'll never know. Nor whether they would have returned. For José immediately began to plan a change of direction.

It was time he went back to Spain for a while. This would keep him away from the Black Hand's clutches and from the demands of the Income Tax department.

And there was another reason. He felt it was time he married. He had told Matilda he would return when he had made money. He was now a man of substance. He would claim his beautiful bride. After the wedding, they could travel in Europe for some time, while the heat went out of his Australian problems.

Then he would return to the Queensland region he had come to love and settle down and have a family.

He had it all planned.

He had underestimated the Australian Taxation officials, who were beginning to catch up with tax dodgers. They were targeting especially, the Southern Europeans who operated in a cash economy, with no receipts and no records of dealings. Many thousands of Italians and Spaniards were putting in false returns or owed large amounts in back payments.

A favourite way to keep away from the Tax Department was to leave Australia for a while, as José was planning. But the tax men were becoming more cunning than their 'clients'. They had recently begun to scan the shipping list of intending passengers to Europe.

Sure enough, there he was.

José Paronella, bound for Barcelona.

Still José was not beaten. He was determined not to pay and equally determined to go back to Spain.

He grew a beard, let his hair grow long and dressed roughly, like a hobo. Then he applied for another passport, with a new photo and using his mother's name. It was all so easy. The passport system was still very casual in Australia.

He then booked another passage under his assumed identity.

Early in 1924, José Buxeda sailed for his native Spain.

Chapter Five

In the summer of 1924, a young Catalan woman, Margarita Soler, was working in France. She was dark haired, with olive skin and a wonderful warm sunny smile. She was twenty two years old.

For the past few years, she had lived with one of her sisters, whilst training as a furrier in one of the fashion houses. She loved her work - the sensuous feel of the fur, the intricate designs of the garments, which looked so fabulous when modeled by the mannequins for wealthy lady customers.

She had even saved enough money to buy some fur off-cuts. Each evening, she had worked from her own design, to make these into a coat for herself. She loved to wear it when boyfriends took her out to dinner.

Margarita was due for holidays and she decided it was time she made a trip back home to La Vall to visit her family.

When she reached her mother's house, she sensed something was wrong. Her mother seemed worried and embarrassed.

"I wish your father was still alive," she kept saying, over and over.

And there was a stranger in the house. Margarita looked at the visitor more carefully. He seemed vaguely familiar.

He smiled at her. "My name's José Paronella."

Then Margarita remembered. She had last seen him in 1911 when she was a 10 year old child. She had known then that he was betrothed to her elder sister, Matilda, but she had never given the matter much thought.

Now she understood her mother's concern. Matilda had not waited for her long gone suitor. She had married three years ago and had a two year old child! José himself had contributed to the problem by not writing to his betrothed or her family during his years in Australia.

"I hate writing letters!" was his only excuse.

Then Margarita saw her mother's crestfallen expression suddenly lift. She smiled at José and turned to Margarita.

"There is a solution. You, Margarita, will marry José Paronella. It will recover our family's honour and provide you with a sound future."

Margarita's mind was in a whirl. It was all happening too suddenly. José was certainly handsome but what would he be like as a husband. He was 14 years older than her. Her mother's voice interrupted her thoughts.

"José has worked very hard in Australia. He is a very wealthy man."

"But will he be kind and thoughtful?" wondered Margarita. She realised he would want her to move with him to Australia. She knew of other local women who had gone there and had heard it wasn't an easy life.

Would she cope with the climate, the strange country, the language - and the loneliness?

"You will be able to come back and visit us often," pleaded her mother. "Think about it, Margarita."

Marriage to José promised adventure, and a future as the wife of a successful man.

And he was very handsome.

The decision was made. Margarita accepted her mother's plan, José agreed to the arrangements and they were betrothed.

José had one problem. He was running short of money and with the wedding and other expenses, he decided to cable his friend Joe Donatui.

*Cable me £500 from my bank account.
Signed Pep de La Vail.*

The Innisfail bank manager was suspicious.
"Who is this Pep? My client's name is José."
Not until Joe explained that José was short for Josép; and Pep was short for Josép, was the manager convinced.
The money was sent and José was financial again.
During the following months, José told Margarita about his plans for their future in Australia. They would be living at first on a cane farm, but soon, he would buy land and begin to build his life's dream - a Spanish castle and pleasure grounds.
The castle would have ornamental balustrades and balconies. Inside there would be a huge ballroom and a restaurant. The grounds would have fountains and pavilions - and beautiful trees and flowers. And a lake for boating and tennis courts, even a bowling rink! People would come from all over the district to visit this wonderful place.
Margarita was entranced by the knowledge and experience of her future husband. He seemed so certain of his ideas and so confident of their success.
On 16th September, 1925, Margarita and José were married in the local Registry Office. As was the Catalan tradition, they returned separately to their family homes. The marriage was not yet to be consummated.
After 3 days, they were married in a traditional church ceremony, with all their family present.
Margarita wore a long white dress, with tiny buttons down the bodice front and short sleeves. Her veil was held in place by a simple hairpiece, decorated with three rows of pearls. She seemed serene and beautiful, alongside her husband, who looked particularly handsome in his grey morning coat, with white shirt and bow tie.
They were now man and wife, legally and in the eyes of the Church.

There followed a period of travel in Europe. José was keen to gather as many ideas as possible. They looked at buildings and gardens; at tourist parks and cinemas, ballrooms and

Wedding photo of Margarita and José

cafes, and even hydro electric schemes. In Madrid, José was particularly interested in the design of the cafe by the pool in the Botanic Gardens.

It was all Margarita could do to keep up with her energetic husband. He seemed driven by some strong force. He had this incredible urge to absorb ideas and information. He never wrote anything down - just stored it all in his mind.

Finally, their 'honeymoon' trip was over. In early 1926, they left Europe and set sail for Australia. Travelling via America, the voyage would last seven weeks.

This was Margarita's first real chance to relax and get to know José in more depth. She had already found out that he had a temper. Their first disagreement had come when she was packing her suitcases ready for the voyage. José sat watching and suddenly he came over and lifted a garment from her carefully packed case.

"What on earth are you taking this to Australia for?"

It was Margarita's cherished fur coat!

It would have been alright if Margarita had given in straightaway. But so upset was she, that she ignored all her early Catalan training about how a wife must obey her husband.

"I made it. I want it with me!"

"You don't have any idea what the climate is like. Give it to one of your sisters."

But Margarita was in tears.

"I could just wear it, now and, again."

José by now was very angry.

"Leave it!" he shouted, pulling the coat from its tissue wrapping and throwing it on the floor"

And in La Vail it had remained.

In all other ways, José had been a kind and loving husband.

There were long periods at sea. They strolled the decks and then settled in a quiet corner and talked. There was so much she wanted to know.

"What's the climate really like? And the countryside?"

José looked across the ocean to the far horizon.

"It's an enormous land, Australia. The hills go on forever and ever and the paddocks stretch as far as you can see, and the sky - on a clear day, it's a wonderful high blue - but, when its raining, it disappears altogether. And the rain falls so heavily you can't hear anything else but the sound of it battering on the tin roof."

Margarita was puzzled. "Tin roof?"

"There aren't many tiled roofs where we're going. They make them of corrugated iron, but they call it 'tin'."

He went on … "And then there are the floods, so deep and strong they can pick up whole logs and carry them away … one bloke had felled some logs at Mena Creek. A flash flood came and away went his logs! Years later, he was picnicking with his children on the Barnard Islands. He came across some logs partially covered in sand. His own brand name was marked on them!"

Margarita loved to hear José talk.

"Tell me some more," she begged.

"Well, in a bad flood, one of the farmers was worried about his chooks - you know, hens, poultry, fowl? So he put them on a few planks nailed together and they were found the next day downstream - all safe and still on their 'raft'."

Margarita laughed.

"What do you most love about life in Queensland?"

José thought carefully.

"I guess it's the easy going friendship. 'Mateship', they call it. You always help another bloke if he's in trouble or has problems. You mightn't even know him, but you still help.

There was a man called Noone, Henry Noone. He had a camp in the South Johnstone area, near Mena Creek - just a slab hut with a dirt floor. He used a couple of rocks with old railway lines over them for a fire for cooking.

A police sergeant had been out in the saddle all day, looking for some Abos who had attacked a settler. He was wet through when he reached Noone's camp and very hungry. Noone invited him in and while he dried himself off, Noone knocked up a damper and cooked it on the fire. The policeman ended up having it with 12 eggs! He reckoned it was the best meal he'd ever had in his life."

"What did you have for meals when you were cutting cane?"

José described the huge quantities of meat, vegetables, pasta and fruit he had eaten.

"You don't seem to have put on much weight," smiled Margarita looking at her fit, athletic husband.

"Who did the cooking?"

"Each team had a cook, usually one of the blokes, or sometimes one of the men was married and his wife would make the meals."

He smiled to himself.

"There's one story worth telling, because it could happen to you!

One of the women was cooking for her husband and the twenty men in his gang. They were very fond of her chicken soup. This particular day, she had a large pot of soup on the open fire, bubbling away. She heard a 'Splotch', looked round but the soup was alright, no soot or anything, so she ignored it.

Awhile later, the men were coming in for lunch. She could hear them 'washing up' on the verandah. She gave the soup a final stir and found half the head and the skin of a goanna. It had fallen down the chimney and into the pan. Desperately she fished around with her slotted spoon, finding some more bits - but the rest of the reptile had cooked into the soup.

With twenty hungry men waiting to be fed, she had no option but to dish up the meal. As her husband came in, she tried to tell him not to eat it, but he was busy chatting and didn't listen.

'Great soup!' called out one of the men."

Margarita wrinkled her nose.

"How horrible!"

Another day, they were lying sunbathing. José was thinking aloud.

"Do you know what I love to hear at the farm? The sound of the Italians singing in the canefields as they work. Their voices are soft on the humid air. I could listen all day."

Margarita was starting to look forward to her new life, though she did have one major worry. She could speak very little English. José had taught her a few words and phrases, but they always spoke Catalan to each other.

A fellow passenger had given her an English phrase book. It was all so strange. She tried to say the words but they came out all wrong and José had to keep correcting her. She was glad, at least, that one of them was familiar with the language.

Their time on the voyage passed all too quickly. Preparations were being made for the ship's arrival in Australia. All their suitcases were repacked and they stood at the rail, watching the coastline come closer and closer.

As they came into harbour, several boats chugged across to meet them and immigration and other officials came on board.

An announcement came over the ship's loudspeaker system:

"Mr and Mrs José Paronella. You are required in the Purser's office immediately"

The Australian official was sitting at a table waiting for them. He was very polite. But what he had to say was a clear and official directive.

"We cannot allow you and your wife to enter Australia."

José knew what the problem was but Margarita was totally in the dark. She looked across at José for reassurance, for explanation.

"It's alright, noia." He put his arm around her "You go back to the cabin while I sort out this misunderstanding."

When Margarita had left, José turned to the official.

"It's about tax, isn't it?"

The Australian nodded.

"You reckon I owe the Australian Taxation Department some money?" The official smiled … "Well, as a matter of fact, you don't owe us anything.

While you were away, we took £1000 from your personal bank account in Innisfail. That makes us even."

José was furious. How dare they take his money, without his permission! And how stupid he had been to come back to Australia using his own passport. Not that he'd had much choice, with his new wife coming on the voyage with him.

He knew that he would have to stay cool, if he was to talk his way back into Australia.

"If I don't owe anything, why can't I return? After all, I am an Australian citizen."

The official looked serious.

"How do we know you won't try to do the same thing again? How can we be sure that you will be an honest citizen in the future?"

"There must be a way I can convince you. I only want to return to my home in South Johnstone and work hard for my wife and hopefully, for my children. You can ask anybody in that area. They will tell you that I am serious. I will not make the same mistake again."

"Is there one particular person who would go guarantor for your good behaviour?" asked the official.

José saw the first ray of hope.

The next day, the officials contacted Joe Donatiu, José's friend and mentor. He was indeed willing to sign the necessary papers, to allow José and Margarita to enter Australia.

"It's all fixed," José told his worried and puzzled wife. And that was the last word he spoke on the subject. And Margarita, relieved that the trouble was over, didn't ask any questions. She trusted José to deal with such official business.

"He knows what he is doing," she reassured herself.

José breathed a sigh of relief. He was becoming pretty good at talking himself out of strife!

Aerial View of Paronella Park

Chapter Six

Within weeks of their arrival back in Australia, José had bought another cane farm. This one was at Mourilyan.

For the first time, Margarita had her own home. The house was typical of cane farms in the region. It was built to suit the climate of high rainfall and humidity.

To make the most of any cooling breeze, the house was set on high timber stumps. The walls were timber clad, the roof corrugated iron. To keep out the glare of the afternoon sun, wooden slatted blinds hung outside the west facing windows.

Underneath was a shady cool area where José would park the car, which he intended to buy. He also put up a clothesline, so Margarita could dry clothes on wet days.

Their lifestyle was physically hard, with all household jobs being done by hand. But Margarita never complained. She was strong and fit; and she knew how much better off she was than earlier Spanish women who had come to live in the sugarcane district.

Their homes had often been no more than a corrugated iron shed - horrendously hot and with little or no ventilation. Inside, hessian sacks divided the space into 'rooms'.

Furniture was makeshift, with beds often no more than a spring supported on 4 wooden boxes.

The kitchen was outside. The family would bathe and the laundry be done in the creek.

Margarita had heard the story of Dolores Donatui, who came from Catalonia to join her husband Claudio in 1914. One day, Dolores was doing the family washing down at the creek. She noticed that leaves were dropping from the tree over her head and falling into the water. She felt the hairs on her neck stand on end. Something had to be wrong. There was no breeze to blow the leaves from the tree - so why the sudden falls? She looked up.

A dozen or more tree snakes were staring down at her!

Margarita was thankful that José had built a small laundry out the back, with a set of wash troughs and a copper. On wash days, she lit the fire under the copper and did all the laundry - clothes, towels, linen. José had also bought her a mangle, which had a handle she turned to press the excess water out of the clothes. She thought herself very fortunate.

They were actually out in the laundry, when Margarita laughingly turned to José:

"I'm so grateful for the laundry, Noi. With all the nappies I'll soon have to wash, it will be of great help."

José stared at her for a moment. Then her message sank in.

He waltzed her out into the garden.

"A baby! A baby! Our very own baby!"

They stopped, breathless.

Later, over a cup of coffee, José couldn't stop talking about their future child.

"Do you realise, our baby will be born Australian. And we'll make sure it speaks both English and Catalan. Because its future is here, even though its roots are in Spain."

Margarita herself still spoke very little English. Whilst working in Europe, she had picked up basic French, but had never anticipated the need for English.

Suddenly, this became very important to her. As much as she loved chatting with Spanish friends and neighbours, she could never be truly accepted as Australian, until she mastered the language.

José spoke fluent, if accented English, learnt in his early years in Australia, talking with fellow cane workers and later, with farmers and businessmen, as he made his fortune.

At that time, there were no English language classes which Margarita could attend. She had no books which would have helped.

A Spanish-speaking migrant told Margarita how she had coped with the language problem.

"It was very, very hard. My husband would work away from home for long periods - he had a camp in the bush. He would send one of his men to me, for fresh provisions. He did not speak Spanish. I knew no English.

So, I would gather all the food tins on the table. Open each in turn and say 'Yes? No?' and the man would say 'Yes. Sugar'. This way, I learnt basic words.

But this was not enough. Then I found a wonderful way to learn. Comics! Each Sunday, there were comic strips inside the newspapers. I pored over these, looking at the pictures and studying the words, to see what the characters were doing. Ginger Meggs and I became great friends!"

Margarita also found the comic strips useful.

But her greatest help was José himself. Though they spoke Spanish together at home, he would frequently help her to understand English words and expressions - and the Australian accent.

There were so many problem words. The men were lining up for their wages. She heard them say it was Pie Day What did they mean? Was this a special time when pies were eaten as a celebration?

And what did they mean when they said: "Old Mick's up the creek"

- when she knew he was out in the paddock?

Gradually, Margarita began to learn the language of her new country.

It would be a long time, however, before she learnt to accept the vast range of native creatures which insisted on sharing their home with them.

Her first encounter had come on her second day She went to use the outside toilet. Sitting staring at her from the toilet seat was an enormous green frog!

Spiders would invade the rooms and the verandah, setting up huge webs, to attract their victims. Margarita was exceptionally clean. Each day she would brush the webs away - by nightfall, they would be back.

In the evening, if you left a door open for a moment, a cloud of moths would fly in, and dance around the lamps. They were not small and dainty, like Spanish moths. They were huge, horrible creatures with an awful smell.

The climate caused Margarita another major problem. Green would grew on everything. José's leather shoes were covered in it and Margarita's handbag, which she had brought from Spain, was ruined. She quickly learned never to leave leather items in dark cupboards, and to constantly bring clothes out into the sun to air.

The North Queensland climate was certainly totally different from anything she had experienced in Europe. She found the combination of heat and high humidity very hard to take.

Fortunately, in the latter months of her pregnancy, the short winter period eased her discomfort, slightly. There was less rain and the temperatures dropped a little.

Locals told her:

"The only difference between Summer and Winter is you may need a sweater."

On the 24th September 1926, Margarita gave birth to a baby girl. She would be christened Teresa Dolores Maria Soler Paronella.

The baby was born at home, with the help of the local midwife. She was born with the 'veil' - the membrane which should have been kept for good luck. Unfortunately, the midwife threw it away - her only comment at the time being:

"Oh, my! What an ugly baby!"

Hardly an encouraging start for the young Teresa.

As the baby grew, Margarita's thoughts turned to the future. What would it be like to bring up children in this new country? She hoped there would be good schools. She didn't want her sons and daughters working on the farm, as so many did, at a very young age. This was the only way some farmers could cope. The whole family worked the farm - children barefooted, burned by the sun. She had heard of one girl, now 18 years old, who had never worn shoes!

Margarita found it very difficult to accept these Australian ways, even though as a child, she herself had lived under similar hardworking conditions.

"It should be different here," she told José.

"You don't know what you want. One minute you want Australia to be different; the next you are longing for Catalan ways!"

Margarita didn't reply She didn't want José to get mad with her again. She knew what he was thinking about. She had been planning for their first Christmas in Australia.

"We'll have all our traditional foods - and it'll be just like home," she told José.

That evening, one of their Australian neighbours had come to visit, bringing a Christmas Cake as a gift. Margarita didn't open the box until after the woman had left. She was horrified.

"That's not a proper Christmas cake. It's heavy and stodgy and full of fruit. I want a Catalan cake, a wonderful light torte, with liquor and cream! We're not going to eat it. Give it to some of your workers."

She had not expected José's angry reaction.

"We will eat it. And you will go to our neighbours and tell them how much we appreciated their gift. It is an Australian Christmas cake. You are an Australian. Eat it."

Margarita had been in tears but she had not dared go against her husband or his temper.

She returned to her role of dutiful wife and now spent her time looking after her new daughter, caring for the house and garden - and worrying about José.

Her husband still spent a lot of time in the canefields, clearing and planting. And he walked long distances, over to Mena Creek, looking for land to buy

There was an old man who did a few odd jobs around the farm. He loved to frighten Margarita with stories about the snakes which hid in the cane; the poisonous rats which could kill a man with one bite; and the mosquitoes which could infect you with a fatal disease.

As he walked away chuckling to himself, Margarita knew that he exaggerated. Yet, such dangers did exist. José came from town one day and told her about a fellow he used to work with, who had died of fever - Weil's disease, they called it.

And then there were cases of malaria, scrub typhus, and various strains of Asian flu.

Margarita prayed that José would stay free of these illnesses.

She also worried on days when José had to go to Innisfail, on business or to buy provisions or tools for the farm. Spanish friends had told her what a wild place it was. The men were making good money and would go into town to drink, gamble and fight over women. There was no shortage of hotels and grog shanties - or of booze. Some even drank Banyan Rum, a concoction made from meths, Condy's crystals and boot polish!

The townspeople were powerless to stop the drunken rampages which even took place during daylight hours.

José and Margarita, with baby Teresa

When José went to town, Margarita waited anxiously all day for his return.

Her worries increased on the days when he went up to Mt Garnet, where he had a mine. In the late 1920's, the way up to the mineral belt was by a treacherous road - unmade, narrow and winding. On corners, three foot high posts separated the lanes, making it difficult to get around without hitting the barrier. The edges of the road frequently broke away and this, plus the poor camber, caused many vehicles to tip off into the scrub.

The road was difficult even in good weather, but in the wet, it was a nightmare.

José had already had one accident, when his vehicle slipped in wet conditions and hit a tree.

José's restlessness was growing. He talked constantly of his plans for building their Spanish castle. He was highly anxious about finding the perfect spot. Nothing short of perfection would satisfy him.

Margarita's fears and concerns for José and their future overshadowed her own loneliness. She took comfort in her pride in José and her love for the baby Teresa.

"Soon, soon," she told herself, "José will find his land."

José and Margarita with Teresa and the family car.

Boating by Mena Creek Falls

Chapter Seven

Mena Creek rises in the mountains at the extreme southern end of the Francis Range. It falls sharply from the high country, then meanders through tropical rainforest before making its spectacular 20 metre drop over the Falls to the waterhole below.

In the years before European settlement, two different aboriginal tribes inhabited the area. One was located along the Camp Creek area, the other camped near the Falls on the southern bank of Mena Creek.

Their trails led along the ridge to Liverpool Creek on the western side of the Basilisk Range. The tracks were narrow and frequently blocked by Wait-a-Whiles and other thorny jungle vines.

The aboriginals were described by locals as "Savage blacks, cannibal types".

In the latter part of the 19th century, a Foot and Mounted Police Base camp was set up on the southern bank of Mena Creek. Records show that on 31st December 1890, 2 constables and 3 native trackers were based there.

The rich timbers in the area, especially the immense stands of red cedar, were soon attracting a lot of attention. There was good money to be made from felling the timber and selling it to the mills.

One particularly successful timber getter was Henry Augustine Noone. He obtained a lease from the government and set up a camp at the top of Mena Creek Falls. This remained his headquarters for two years as he felled the cedar and hauled it out from the tropical bush.

Whilst working in the area, Noone came to love the topography and above all, Mena Creek with its safe swimming hole. And the dramatic falls.

Noone wanted to buy land in this beautiful spot, but he realised that the government would not be interested in the odd one or two blocks, with all the survey costs involved.

He turned the problem over and over in his mind. In what situation would the government sell blocks? Only if there were enough people in one area willing to be involved in clearing and developing the land.

Noone had experience in surveying and so he did the basic survey work himself. Only then did he approach the authorities. He had already spoken to many other men and so was able to assure the government that if the whole area was divided into 40 blocks, each of about 160 acres, then he already had applicants for each block. The officials were convinced; the official surveys completed and the Settlement Scheme proclaimed.

Noone himself was assigned Portion 56 on the southern side of Mena Creek. He set up a more permanent camp, with shelter for himself and an area for his horse.

He often brought his family from Innisfail out to his camp for a picnic and a swim. His son, Dan Noone, recalls wonderful days spent swimming naked under the falls and, eating huge meals of camp tucker: damper and cornbeef, washed down with billy tea.

Eventually Noone cleared an area alongside the creek and gave it to the local council for use as a picnic and recreation reserve.

His love of the falls led him to make further developments on his land. He wrote in his diary: "The water flowing over Mena Creek Falls was a great attraction to me always. The idea of being able to put it to some use was always in my mind, and apart from living near it and using it personally, I wanted more people to enjoy it."

With sound business sense, Noone knew there was a demand for a hotel and accommodation in the area.

'During the winter school holidays numbers of Tablelands people came to Mena Creek and pitched tents; they all claimed the swimming was the attraction.'

On 3rd October 1928, Noone began clearing the land for his hotel site. That summer

Mena Creek Falls

proved to be particularly hot, slowing down building work. Yet, in early 1929, the Mena Creek Hotel opened for business. Noone's dreams and careful plans were coming to fruition.

While all this was happening, another inventive mind was looking at Mena Creek.

The area fascinated José Paronella. Its visual beauty was awe-inspiring. After miles and miles of sugarcane and low flat rolling country, to suddenly come upon the dense green of the tropical vegetation, the flowing creek, then the dramatic falls and the safe swimming hole below.

He stood on the banks of Mena Creek. It was the perfect spot to put his dream into action; to build his Spanish castle and pleasure grounds, blending the buildings with the tropical vegetation and plantings of exotic trees and shrubs.

He could see the finished park in his mind, in complete and accurate detail. His castle would rest on the rocky cliff, with a cafe and pavilion at the lower level. There would be streams and bridges; paths bordered with stone walls; tennis courts and gardens; and always the visual backdrop of the magnificent falls.

Somehow, he had to buy land here. But how? The southern bank was owned by Noone, who already had his own plans for further development - a hall for community use and shops and dwellings. It was obvious that Mena Creek's township would develop on that southern side.

That left the northern bank. José walked and climbed over the whole area. It was virgin rainforest near the falls, a tangle of tropical trees, vines and creepers. From there, a steep escarpment dropped to the creek level.

Apart from Mena Creek, another stream ran through the area, arising from an artesian spring and falling about 14 feet into a small rock pool. It then flowed down a steep sided valley to join Mena Creek further south.

Near the junction of the creeks, the land flattened out into a flood plain, grassed for cattle grazing. The land then rose again, to level out where the sugar fields began.

José began to make enquiries. The whole property on this side of the creek was held by a Mr August Frederick Koppen. It was under a Deed of Grant of Land, given on 7th November 1923.

Half the acreage was already under sugarcane, and Koppen was continuing to clear more of the undulating section each year

José was becoming highly anxious. This was the perfect place for his dream. But he was very doubtful whether Mr Koppen would sell. After all, he had developed his farm, built a comfortable house and settled his family in the district.

Then, José saw a possible solution. He went to see Mr Koppen.

The family were all there when he arrived. After formal handshakes and the offer of a drink, José sat down at the kitchen table opposite August Koppen and put his carefully thought out proposition.

"Mr Koppen. There is an area of your land which you do not and never can use - the South West corner. It is all gullies and falls. It's too rough. You can never grow cane on it."

Mr Koppen nodded, his face giving nothing away.

"Would you sell me that piece of land? I can pay you cash. You would then have money to help develop the usable parts of your property."

Koppen sat for several minutes without responding.

Then, to José's immense, though disguised joy, Mr Koppen agreed to José's proposition.

It only remained to settle the exact area and the price.

August Koppen would sell José 12 acres, 2 roods and 29 perches - for a price of £120.

José walked away from the Koppen house, back to Mena Creek. He sat down facing the tumbling falls. It was early evening and the bush had quietened.

José crossed himself.

"This is the most beautiful place on earth!"

Later, he rose and walked the 14 miles back to Mourilyan to tell Margarita his news.

Mena Creek Falls at Paronella Park

Chapter Eight

To understand José's dream and the driving force of his ambition, one aspect cannot be underestimated. He was a Catalonian.

And that is not the same as being Spanish.

The predominant culture of Spain stems from Castillian traditions. It is the most popular image of flamenco guitar music, flamboyant dance and vivid, colourful costumes. We think of their pleasure in food and wine; their addiction to bullfighting; and their warm, outwardly demonstrative nature.

José, the Catalan, did not come from this tradition.

Catalonians see themselves as European, rather than Spanish. The Province, indeed, lies in the North East of Spain, bordering France to the north, Aragon to the west and the Mediterranean on the east.

Catalonia has a strong legacy of independence, holding on to its own laws, traditions and language.

A kind of fierce determination flows through Catalonian people.

'El Catalan de las piedras sacs pan.'

'The Catalan will get bread from stones.'

They have a fundamental belief in trade and business and see hard work and long hours as the way to success.

Their business acumen is often put down to the extensive Jewish element. Jewish families arrived steadily in the region after the Diaspora. Over the years, they became increasingly resented and were finally expelled by Catholic monarchs Fernando and Isabel, but not before their influence had permeated Catalan life through intermarriage, through business and financial practices and through the adoption by Catalonians of many Jewish trade abilities and skills.

Catalonia is proud of this Jewish heritage.

The people are also conservative and sober in dress and deportment.

They do not drink heavily. It is, even now, common for a group of Catalonians to share a bottle of wine over dinner and not to even finish it.

There is no bullfighting tradition - in fact, the 'sport' is actively disliked.

There is no strong Macho ideal.

Nor do they share the Spanish tastes in music and dance. Flamenco is replaced by the traditional group dance La Sardana, performed every Sunday in villages and cities throughout the region.

Catalonians are distrusted and not generally liked by the rest of the Spanish population. They are regarded as being only interested in money; as being greedy and mean. They have a reputation for being secretive, clannish and hostile to outsiders.

The Catalan sees himself as being, both literally and figuratively, closer to Geneva than Seville.

This was José's heritage - European ideals, belief in hard work and business; in sober behaviour and family values, with no desire to waste time and money on frivolous pursuits.

These qualities were to enable José to achieve the practical aspects of his ambitious dream.

José's verbal agreement with August Koppen for the Purchase of the land ran into legal delays. Koppen held the property under the Lands Act 1910-1929 and before he could sell, he had to surrender his parcel of land back to the state. He would then be issued with a new Deed of Grant of Land. Only then could he subdivide and complete the sale to José.

Whilst these legal procedures were taking place, Koppen agreed to allow José to begin clearing work - but no building. The sale was not finalised until 21st July 1931.

At last the project could begin in earnest. José had built his home and castle so many times in his head that his plans and ideas were ready to be put into immediate action.

Obtaining the right materials was always going to be a problem. He would need to use as much from the property itself as he could. Otherwise, inevitable delays, waiting for items from Innisfail or Cairns, could hold up the job for weeks.

There was plenty of sand and gravel in the creek. José had planned to start building up at the road level; a cottage for his family, for Margarita and baby Teresa.

How were the sand and gravel to be brought up to the higher level? There was only one answer. It would all have to be carried up, manually, using a yoke and buckets. José shook his head.

"This will be impossible, considering the steep incline."

José never gave up on a difficult problem. He ran it over and over in his mind. Then, the solution came. He would work into his design, a set of steps - a kind of cement staircase.

Tons of gravel and sand were laboriously carried up the newly-cut steps, and later, down the steps went bags of cement and hundreds of yards of steel reinforcing.

The best sand was in the centre of the creek. José acquired a flat-bottomed boat. The sand had to be lifted into the boat and then taken over to the bank, before beginning its long trip up the steps.

Next José needed cement, and in huge quantities. He knew there was none produced in the local area. It was imported from Germany in huge three hundred weight casks. Inevitable, it absorbed moisture on the voyage and still more on its way from ship to Mena Creek. It would need to be gauged carefully, to make a strong mixture.

The next problem was to obtain metal to reinforce the structures. Fortunately there was an abundant supply of discarded rails from the canefields - ones which had bent or buckled - or were going rusty.

There was no shortage of suitable timber. There were several abandoned houses in the district and it was accepted that anyone who needed materials would simply take them. José went down to the old Bianchi house near the dip, only a short distance away, and helped himself to framework timber for his cottage. For the concrete formwork, he used old six inch wide tongue and groove flooring.

What José could never have known was the tragic fact that he was building into his structures basic weaknesses. Years later, these defects would cause much of his work to crumble.

The first problem concerned the building materials he took from Mena Creek. In this area, the sand had a very high mica content. By structure, mica has a flat, slippery cleavage plane which bonds very poorly with the burnt limestone of cement.

Over a period of time, it allows water to penetrate into the cured concrete, leeching away the cement and weakening the whole structure.

The water also caused the steel to rust and consequently to expand, causing internal cracks and breakdown.

In many places, the old mill rails would also prove too thick, compared to the amount of concrete around them - sometimes as little as one inch.

Nor did José add strength to his concrete structures by adding filings or aggregate.

José was blissfully unaware of these future problems. He was intent on finding his next material. He was planning to stucco the outside of his buildings, so he needed a supply of clay to mix with cement to make the slurry. This would then be applied to all external walls by hand.

He had already studied the geology of his property and knew that the best source of clay was the base of a ridge which crossed the land. He would dig into this hillside and take out clay, making a cave.

When he investigated further, he found that the distance straight through the ridge was 42 metres. On the far side was a small creek and a tiny waterfall.

His plan extended dramatically. He would tunnel through the ridge, using the clay as he went. He put out of his mind the fact that all this heavy clay would have to be carried up the 47 steps!

So now he had his supply of timber, sand, gravel, cement and clay.

José believed in having the best available tools. Unfortunately, in his day, only basic manual equipment was available, such as shovels, picks and trowels, amber and bush saws and steel wheeled barrows. He did, fortunately, obtain a cement mixer.

He had no intention of doing all the work himself. He knew the extent of his plans and realistically admitted he would need a variety of helpers.

He told Margarita:

"They will have to be men used to working in hot moist conditions. And who won't mind long hours."

Who better than canecutters? He went over to the hotel.

Maltese Joe was leaning on the counter. He had olive skin, dark wavy hair and the broad strong shoulders which came from his hours in the cane paddocks.

José bought him another beer. He needed this man. Before migrating to Australia, Joe had worked as a skilled carpenter.

"Want a job? I could use you for a year or so, helping with building. You could take a break from canecutting."

Joe looked thoughtful.

"Wouldn't mind. . . but I've got my sister's boy with me."

"I could use him, too - so long as he's willing to work hard." Joe eased himself off the bar stool.

"Pay us cash? No records?"

José nodded.

"OK You've got yourself a couple of helpers."

And the deal was sealed with a handshake.

José was also aware of another source of cheap labour - the unemployed. In the Southern parts of Australia, the Depression was beginning to bite deep. It led to a great influx of men into Queensland, where the depression had not had the same devastating effects. Places like Innisfail and Mourilyan were inundated. A rough shed was erected in Innisfail as a temporary shelter for these homeless unemployed. It was soon full to overflowing and there was nowhere else for them to go.

José, always the shrewd businessman, considered the situation.

'I'll offer them somewhere to sleep and good food, in exchange for work. But I won't pay them wages.'

Some of the unemployed resented this. There was talk amongst themselves.

"He's exploiting us. It'll be like slave labour."

"I don't have many options. I'm single, so there's only one day's work a week for me with the local council. I can't survive on the 10 shillings they pay."

"I still reckon it's a rip-off!"

One younger bloke stood up.

"I'm going over to work for Paronella. At least I'll see some result for the work I do. I'll be helping build something."

In the following months, others were to follow his example.

Finally, José needed men with expertise. He contacted plumbers to assist with water installations, pumps and drains; carpenters to work on roofing and flooring; electricians to do the wiring.

His plans, so long in his mind, were now coming to life before his eyes. As well as working long hours himself, José kept a close control on all the current projects which were on the go at the same time.

Each day he would show the workmen what he wanted doing.

"Watch! I'll show you what we are going to build today."

Using the ancient Egyptian method, José had a shallow tray full of damp sand. He smoothed this flat and then drew his design for that day - a set of steps with equal risers, or the wall of a fountain, or ornamental balustrading for a bridge.

Sometimes there was confusion among his workers over length and height. José worked in the metric measurements, which were familiar to him from his childhood.

José would become exasperated by their mistakes.

"A metre, a metre!" he would indicate with his hands. "It's this long."

All his major buildings were modular, with the similar structures repeated over and over. This may have been part of José's design, but more likely it stemmed from using the same formwork for every job.

Once the basic work for the staircase was completed, José was at last able to start on a dwelling for his family. This was urgently needed so that Margarita and baby Teresa could move in. And he would save so much time, without the long journeys to and from Mourilyan. He would be able to start early and finish late.

The cottage under construction at the top of the cliff

The spot they had chosen for their home was close to the top of the Falls, on a rocky plateau. His plan was basic and simple. He decided to work this one time, in a European rather than a Spanish design. There would be time later for castles and turrets.

He planned to build four main rooms, a bathroom and an entrance hall. These were to be divided off by timber partitions. Above would be an attic area for extra space. The roof would be high pitched with dutch gables and with dormer windows. He would cover it in corrugated iron, which came out in ships from England.

Margarita was worried about how hot it would be under the roof.

José reassured her:

"It'll be OK Noia. I've seen other houses where it works. Besides, I'm putting in windows for cross-ventilation."

Access to the attic was through a 6x4 foot manhole, with a fold-down Ladder.

The foundations were uncomplicated - a layer of sand on the bedrock and a layer of cement. Then, a timber framework with mortared stone for the external walls. He planned later to stucco the surface, but for now, such refinements would have to wait.

The windows were casement style, framed in timber, with deep window reveals.

He fitted up a kitchen in one of the main rooms, with a fuel stove. Later, this would be replaced with a Benzine stove, then a kero and finally, with an electric range.

And, he installed running water. For drinking, this came from the small spring on the property, which José had now named after baby Teresa.

He fitted up a ram pump, which worked by water pressure. Once he started it up, it just went on and on.

José's house had the first indoor plumbing in the region.

"I don't want my Margarita struggling, like other wives, carrying water for cooking and washing."

His wife and family would be looked after. They would have the best he could provide.

Years later, his daughter Teresa, would boast to school friends that she had had a hot shower. This, at a time when most homes thought themselves lucky to have a cold outdoor shower and chip heaters were only just coming in!

The cottage, completed

José attached a laundry at the rear of the house.

All lighting was by kerosene lamps.

José had promised Margarita their new home would be ready for Christmas - and on Christmas Eve, less than three months after laying the foundations, they moved in.

That first night, José and Margarita lay in bed, entranced by the sound of the water from the Falls.

José stroked Margarita's hair.

"Noia. Noia. What wonderful music to make love by."

He was supremely happy. The first stage of his dream was now a reality.

Mena Creek Falls from José's Picnic Area

The Lower Refreshment Rooms

Chapter Nine

With the house complete, José wanted Margarita to have some help with cleaning and cooking and looking after the baby.

"I can cope, José," Margarita insisted.

"Maybe, if you only had the home to see to. But soon, we will have visitors and I will need your help. We must find a girl to live in."

José's friends, the Salleras brothers, recommended a young girl of Spanish parentage. Her name was Montserrat Gabasa, known as Monnie. She was just 15 years of age and it was her first job, apart from helping on her parents' farm.

"I was the housemaid. But really, I just did whatever needed doing - cleaning, washing, ironing, looking after Teresa. On weekends, when visitors began coming to the park, I took the money at the gate and then helped Margarita with afternoon teas."

Monnie shared a bedroom in the cottage with Teresa. She enjoyed the work, except for one or two things.

"I have a terrible fear of snakes and sometimes I would come on one suddenly, as it slithered onto a path to sun himself."

She also hated it when the chooks were killed and she had to help clean and pluck them.

"I could never bring myself to eat chicken again!"

José could now concentrate on the building, with less worry about Margarita and the baby.

Soon after Monnie had settled in, José came into the house after work one day, to find a young visitor. He thought that Monnie had brought a boyfriend to the house and he felt his anger rising.

"Mr Paronella. May I introduce my brother, Richard." José offered his hand in greeting.

They sat down at the kitchen table and Monnie served coffee. José took an instant liking to the tall, enthusiastic young man.

"How would you like to come and live here and help me with the building?"

Richard agreed and moved in to live with the Paronella's. He helped José with whatever work was on the go. They would start each day after breakfast, at about 7.00am and work through until 5.00pm or even later. Some days, darkness caught up with them before they had finished floating a section of concrete. Then, Margarita would be called to hold a lamp while the men completed the job.

By now, work had begun on the ornamental balustrades and the concrete picnic tables and seats by the waterside. These were placed to catch the best view of the falls. Soon after, the building of the cafe began.

In later years, Richard Gabasa never forgot this period of the building work.

"The hardest part was carrying the cement from the top down to the lower level, where we were working. We had to manhandle it down all them steps. I must have counted them a million times. 13 and a rest; 13 and another rest; 13 again. Then 8 to the bottom." Ironically, they were beginning to call it 'The Grand Staircase'.

José now needed more of the clay from his planned tunnel and so digging began in earnest. Richard recalls:

"We did that between us, José and I. We loosened the clay with a pickaxe and shoveled it into a barrow and wheeled it out. It was mostly soil. There was very little rock in that ridge at all."

How did they hold it up?

"We didn't. We were relying on God to help us out - until we could put in the timber formwork and pour the cement."

Didn't he worry?

"Yes, of course I did! Every time we went into the tunnel, I would see Maltese Joe cross himself, in case we didn't come out again!"

The final plan was to go right through to the other side.

"We also dug some side sections where the clay was particularly good. José was going to use these for an aquarium or for showcases. He was always coming up with new ideas."

Richard found José to be a tremendously hard worker.

"He worked non-stop, pausing only to issue an instruction in his loud, raspy voice or to make a new drawing in the sandbox, so that we knew what to do next. But I still enjoyed working alongside him. He was a fine man - courteous to everybody."

The two formed a good team. Both dressed in khaki shorts and shirt, and dark brown from the tropical sun, they struggled against the heat and rain, to bring José's fantasy into reality.

Though José had chosen a basic European design for his home, he had vastly different ideas planned for his other buildings.

He wanted to suggest the fantasy of a Spanish castle, echoing the kind of architecture he had so much admired in his native Catalonia. He had become familiar with the work of one man in particular - the Spanish architect, Antonio Gaudi.

Like José, Gaudi came from a family of humble social status. His father and grandfather worked as coppersmiths. Gaudi always maintained that the legacy from his 'pot and kettle-making' heritage was the main reason why he saw forms directly in space. He solved architectural problems without needing graphic plans. It seems that José also had the same ability to think in space. His mind was his drawing board.

Gaudi's work shows a strong desire to naturalise architecture and to blend it with the surrounding landscape. He wrote about one building:

'The patina of the stone is enriched by the flowers and climbing plants on the balconies, which have given a constantly varied colour to the building.'

Gaudi would no doubt have approved of José's more humble but no less beautiful designs.

José's work also shows strong Moorish influence from Spain, especially in the castellated rooflines, the ballustraded fencing, with square planter pots at the corners. The single columns, which José placed in the picnic area, are similar to those in the Alcazar garden in Seville.

At other times, José designed specifically to suit the tropical climate; to shield out the sun or allow for the movement of cooling breezes.

Though most of the building work progressed smoothly, there were

Mena Creek Falls from the Picnic Area

occasional incidents which underlined the element of danger in all they did.

On one occasion, José had borrowed some horses to haul a grader. He was unhitching them at the end of the day, when the grader suddenly broke loose and rolled forward. Before anyone could react, it rolled over the edge into a deep volcanic drop hole near the carpark. And it is still there to this day. They tried in vain to recover it but the hole is filled with water. They dropped a line with a weight on it. It went down and down, and never reached the bottom.

José went over to the owner of the equipment to return the horses.

'There's just one problem, Pedro. We've lost your grader"

José grumbled later to Margarita: "It'd have been cheaper to buy my own grader in the first place. Now I've had to pay Pedro for the loss of his and haven't even got one of my own!"

The local wildlife also caused a few scary moments. Richard slept in a shed at the far end of the grounds, near the chook house. One night, he was woken by a noisy rumpus. He went into the chook run to investigate and that was his almost fatal mistake. Six or seven snakes had slithered into the run, looking for a meal of tasty young chicken. They lashed out at Richard and coiled angrily between him and the way out. Fortunately, José kept an old cane knife in the run, and Richard holding the hurricane lamp in one hand, slashed away with his free hand, killing some and forcing others to move away, so that he could escape and raise the alarm.

José and his helpers were now working on the cafe building. On his visit to Spain in 1924, José had been to the Botanical Gardens in Madrid. There he had been entranced by their Cafe by the Water. Though he modified this design in his mind, it was the inspiration for the Paronella Park Cafe by the Pool.

The style was romantic and very Spanish. He used his favourite formed concrete structure but decorated the basic shapes with ballustrades and castellations.

The outside was stuccoed with a mortar and clay rough render applied to the moulded concrete by hand. To this day, the imprints of José's hand can be seen pressed into the surface. The original colour was the rich red of the local soil. José later found that the colour washed out. From then on the buildings were white-washed annually to prevent the growth of mildew and improve their appearance.

On the second level of the cafe and reached by sets of steps up each side, was a roof garden. From tables set out in this area, visitors enjoyed a new vista of the gardens as well as catching the cooling breezes. At the back of the roof garden was a small room with a roof balcony above it. Again, this was reached by external stairs.

Inside, the timber tables were

José on his Grand Staircase

The Cafe by the Pool and the small Pavilion

covered with bright check cloths with fresh flowers. Coloured lights ran around the service area. Spanish style pillars supported the roof. On the walls were pictures of Spanish ladies in traditional costume.

The cafe also provided food service for the picnic tables by the pool.

Along each side of the cafe, José built a row of changing cubicles, ten on each side, for male and female swimmers.

A toilet block was now essential - but even this was to be no ordinary utility building. The Spanish theme continued with a roof top balcony and balustraded railings.

To this cafe area, José was later to add a pavilion, in the same castle style. Again, there was a rooftop balcony that was occasionally used for bands of musicians who played for dancers on summer evenings. It also acted as a spectator stand for the frequent tennis tournaments which would be held immediately in front of it.

In 1932, whilst all this intense building activity was going on, Margarita was again pregnant. On 26th August she gave birth to a baby boy, christened Joséph Peter Antone Paronella. This time, Margarita went to the hospital in Innisfail for the birth. José was left to look after Teresa, who was now almost six years old.

Teresa remembers her brother's birth with great fondness; for instead of cooking meals at home, José took her to the hotel - a very rare treat.

Once Margarita and the new baby were settled back home, José was anxious to push on with the next stage of his building plan.

This was to be his 'piéce de résistance' - a Spanish-style castle tower. Some people saw this as José's pure personal folly - a self-indulgent structure satisfying his own dreams. It had, in fact, a valid, practical purpose. It would attract tourists by its visual impact, clearly seen from the main road.

This, like the other buildings, was to be of poured concrete construction, plastered by hand to give a rough textured finish. It would have several levels, with all staircases external, except from ground to first floor.

The support columns were relatively slender, with capitals and a broadening at the top. They resembled many such columns José had seen in Spanish villas.

From the balconies, balustrading was constructed with the top rail fairly dominant and the uprights cast in classic Spanish design. There was a cantilevered second floor balcony and a rooftop balcony, with additional squared pots on the balustrade supports.

The windows and door openings had deep reveals and ornamental heads.

A complex design - but the total effect was magical - a romantic fairytale castle set against the deep green of the tropical jungle. An enchanted place.

At the front, José planned a cool, inviting entrance, rather like an Italian loggia. It was roofed with a pergola structure, covered in bamboo. Tropical hanging orchids, and ferns and palms gave a soft green backdrop. In the centre was a circular fountain pool, stocked with goldfish. The shade and the sound of the water gave a sense of peaceful tranquility.

Visitors could climb to each level of the tower - stopping on the way to look at José's small museum. Here he would collect the most mixed, unusual set of objects; everything from wood samples, raw and polished stones, a coin collection, old firearms, seashells, to a collection of the visiting cards of people from every nation in the world, who would come to see José's castle and be mesmerised by its unusual beauty.

A further set of steps led to the very top of the tower. This gave a view over the park, the falls and pool, lawns and shrubs and beyond to the purple hills in the distance.

José often came up here at the end of the day to look quietly at the beauty of nature and to consider his handiwork. These were, for him, moments of incredible peace.

Monnie Gabasa, meanwhile, was proving indispensible to Margarita, especially now that the new baby had arrived. She freed her from the basic chores so that Margarita could do what she enjoyed most - cooking, caring for the children and - gardening.

For Margarita had fallen in love with the tropical vegetation. She wanted to help José with his plans for the grounds - to herself grow the ferns and orchids and colourful creepers.

And the gardens were indeed beginning to take shape. The paths were formed - straight and formal, in contrast to the kalaedoscopic randomness of the surrounding vegetation.

View of the Castle from the terraced lawns

At night, when the children were asleep, she and José sat in the porch in the cooling evening, as he explained his ideas for the park.

"The paths must intersect and lead our visitors to all areas of the grounds, so that they can wander from one side to another, never tiring of the variety of plants and trees."

And the visitors were already beginning to come, to enjoy not only the walks but the falls, the swimming, and to relish the wonderful afternoon teas.

Margarita made all the cakes and scones herself. Monnie helped by cutting sandwiches and taking the trays down to the tables set either near the house or down by the water's edge.

"Margarita was very particular about everything. She was exceptionally clean and tidy I had to set my trays 'Just so!'.

I didn't wear a uniform - just a simple cotton dress and an apron - Oh, and of course, stockings! They were so hot and sweaty in that climate but it was the correct dress."

Monnie recalls some famous people coming to visit. They had heard already of the beauty of the Spanish style Park and wanted to see for themselves.

"The cyclist Hubert Opperman came, with Nicholas, the Aspro man."

Another day, a car pulled up and a priest and three nuns climbed out. They wanted to have afternoon tea - down on the lower level near the water. Margarita prepared some special cakes and Monnie carried the food and teas down to them.

"We'll tell you when you can collect the trays," said the priest.

Monnie returned to the house and went on with the ironing, dampening the starched linen, and working with two irons, one heating on the stove, while she worked with the other.

Suddenly, José burst in, laughing so much he had to stop for breath before he could tell them.

"It's the priest and nuns. We were working further along the creek. I had my binoculars with me for bird watching, as usual. I looked across and couldn't believe my eyes!"

Margarita crossed herself.

"Oh, no! Not that! Not here!"

José shook his head.

A romantic view of the Castle tower

"No! Not what you are thinking. They were playing on the grass like a group of boisterous children - rolling down the hill, nuns' habits flying all over the place, laughing uproariously - and chasing each other and playing hide and seek!"

Monnie and Margarita joined in his amusement.

Margarita's gentle tolerance came through as she commented:

"You know, they really do have to let off steam sometimes. It's good they can do it so - innocently."

A few minutes later, the priest and three demure nuns returned to the Entrance.

"You can collect the trays now. Thank you so much. We'll come back again."

José smiled.

"Do that, Father. Anytime."

The Top Gardens from across the Falls

Teresa Falls

Chapter Ten

Thomas Edward Alford had the important title of Chief Inspector of Machinery, Scaffolding, Weights and Measures.

In 1934, he made an official visit to Paronella Park. He was to check the safe and correct installation of a piece of machinery - the turbine for José's hydro-electric scheme.

It was not the kind of inspection he made every day. This scheme was, in fact, the first such project ever attempted in Queensland, possibly in Australia.

In the South Johnstone Shire at this time, mains power was only just beginning to come through. It was unreliable, with frequent breakdowns. And it only serviced the major townships, certainly not the smaller villages and outlying farms. Kero lamps were their only form of lighting; cooking was done on fuel stoves.

Whilst in Europe, José had been fascinated by the various hydro-electric schemes which were being constructed. He never dreamt that one day he would construct his own. The ideas stayed in his mind, however, until the day he first saw Mena Creek Falls.

'I could use the power of this water. It is a perfect place to construct a hydro plant.'

The idea of generating his own electricity occupied José's mind constantly during

Block and Tackle system used to lower the Hydro parts into place

The Hydro Parts being lowered into the building

A section of the hydro-electric plant being delivered

1933, as he worked on his building projects or tree plantings. The weather was often unsuitable for outside jobs. 1933 was one of the wettest years in a wet district. He had plenty of time to think.

How would he deal with the problems? Was the flow of water sufficient to do the job? Would he need to dam the flow - and where? How strong would the piers need to be, to support the generator and other equipment? How could he control the flow of power?

Despite all these questions, he was convinced that the scheme would work.

His friends, however, were very sceptical.

"Your ideas are too difficult, too ambitious!"

José, as usual, was ahead of his time. Such situations he saw as an exciting challenge. He was not a man to turn aside from difficult tasks.

He went over to the Mill at South Johnstone and asked to speak to their electrical engineers.

"I want to build this hydro scheme to harness the power from Mena Creek Falls. I know what I want to do, but I don't have any technical knowledge. Will you help me?"

The engineers were at first incredulous but once they realised that José really had thought through the whole concept, they agreed to help. Catching his enthusiasm and optimism, they gave him detailed instructions and promised later to help with the actual installation of the turbine and generator After much thought, consultation and planning, José began to order parts and equipment.

And at last the work could begin.

José had worked out how to dam the flow from Mena Creek. There was an ideal spot, a rocky bar which had been a ford, before the bridge was built. To this he added concrete and stone work.

Then he built a U-shaped aqueduct from the top of the Falls across to the inlet pit.

Through natural gravity, the water fell 30 feet. This was well within the capacity of his turbine which was designed to work with falls up to 500 feet. It was capable of generating far more than the 25 KVA capacity of the alternator.

The turbine itself was quite a sophisticated English model. It had variable pitch inlet valves to control the flow. There was a 24 inch discharge pipe down to the creek to prevent the platform being eroded by the downward rush of water from the turbine. The turbine ran at 500 rpm.

The DC generator was directly coupled to it. This was ex-army stock and acquired quite cheaply.

A governor controlled the speed of the turbine and consequently the frequency of the current and voltage. This was belt driven and changed the angle of the flow of water over the turbine blades, to maintain a constant speed of rotation.

The system ran automatically.

The turbine itself was shaft-connected to a large steel flywheel, which drove a 415 volt AC 3 phase alternator and its 110 volt DC exciter.

The most difficult task of all was the construction of the 12 steel reinforced concrete piers to support the foundation for the turbine house. These had to be set into rock at the base of the falls.

It was necessary to set the turbine and alternator on the concrete platform before the walls and roof were completed.

The turbine and alternator were lowered over the cliff, using a primitive crane system, called 'sheer legs'. The two timber legs were tied together, anchored to the ground and a hook and pulley were used to lower the heavy equipment over the side and down to their position.

Then the walls and roof were built around them.

Access to the turbine house was via a set of very narrow, steep concrete steps.

This meant that the turbine could never be removed from its position.

José also installed a holding tank and gate valve, a pipe to the Falls weir and a strum box behind the weir to filter stones and debris.

It was a safe and manageable system.

This D/C power system generated electricity which could be used, but not stored. But José certainly had plenty of plans for using his new resource.

He would reticulate the system throughout the park and down to the tunnel to supply lighting. It would drive pumps to transfer water from Teresa Creek up to the holding tank above the house. He would use it to power refrigeration.

Above all, he wanted the D/C for the carbon arcs in the picture theatre he had planned.

And on that important day when Thomas Edward Alford arrived for his inspection - what was the verdict?

"I have a great deal of respect for you, Mr Paronella and for what you are trying to create. It is admirable that you are attempting ..."

His voice went on and on.

José waited in the greatest suspense. What was the answer? Yes? or No?

"... And I will report that your system is absolutely safe and that you can now generate your own electricity."

To Mr Alford's astonishment, José grabbed him around the waist and swung him into an impromptu dance.

"Thank you! Thank you! Now we will have lights - everywhere!"

The first night that the hydro-electric system was

José's hydro-electric plant, seen from the pool area

operating, José lay in bed listening to two beautiful sounds - the water cascading over Mena Creek Falls and the hum of his hydro-electric plant.

One more part of his dream had come to fruition.

José's Spanish Castle

Paronella Park from across the falls

Chapter Eleven

When the Moors invaded and occupied Spain in the 8th century, they brought with them their political ideology and their religious ideals. They also brought their ability to create beautiful gardens and parks.

Their landscape designs linked closely to Muslim beliefs. The aesthetically pleasing Moorish gardens contained secluded, quiet places which encouraged meditation.

They believed that Nature should never be overridden by man's creations. Buildings and all man-made structures in a garden should be designed as part of the landscape, with no sharp divisions between man's creations and natural features.

Nor should there be sharp symmetries in the design. Nature itself is anything but symmetrical and so to design rigid lines is an insult to Nature and displeasing to Allah.

The whole garden should be a source of daily pleasure, leading with gentle continuity from section to section, from vista to vista.

Their hot, dry climate led to another design element - their use of water for fountains, small streams and waterfalls. These added beauty to the gardens and soothed the senses by their sound. They also cooled the air and made the water seem more abundant.

The Spanish Moorish gardens often included a special private paradise, a Glorietta - this was an arbor usually thickly draped with creepers.

When on his visit to Spain, José made an effort to see as many private villa gardens as he could.

One afternoon, Margarita was tired.

"Do we really have to see this garden? It's a long way. It's getting late."

But José would not be put off.

They also looked at the larger Pleasure Parks in cities such as Barcelona and Madrid. Whilst echoing the tranquility aspects of the smaller gardens, these Parks also included activities to entertain the visitors - boating, music, gentle sports and relaxing cafés.

This background of Spanish Moorish design was to underlay many of José's concepts and plans. Yet he was to take their ideas and mould them to his own dream.

He, too, wanted to create a Park which would be a retreat from the everyday world; a place where spirit and soul could relax. But his Park, unlike those of more arid climates, would provide an oasis, not from the desert, but from the acres and acres of sugarcane which surrounded his gardens.

He would create an exotic fantasy world, a fairyland with romantic castles, dark tunnels, streams and bridges and a secret garden. There would be mystery and surprise.

His creation was unique. It blended Spanish architecture with the Queensland bush; a stretch of naturally beautiful land was changed by man - and in the process, its impact enhanced; its contrasts emphasised.

José also fulfilled the second part of his dream - his grounds would be a Pleasure Park, a place where his visitors could swim or stroll, play tennis or bowls, enjoy a relaxed meal. They could sit quietly in the Secret Garden or enjoy the company of others at the tables by the pool. They could dance in the ballroom or rest in the loggia - at all times surrounded by the beauty of his Park.

None of this happened accidentally. It was the result of much observation, thought, discussion and planning.

"I don't want Paronella Park to be a haphazard collection of activity areas and thoughtless plantings," José told Margarita.

He had to face the problem of giving the grounds unity and continuity, without boredom. His design would have to hold together various sections and functions.

He would do this by underlining certain elements - the use of water, the tropical nature of the vegetation and the romantic castellated style of his buildings and garden bridges and walls.

Then he would introduce contrasts. His guests would be presented with a variety of vistas, each differing in height and perspective; in intimacy or openness. He would design his plantings to create variety in light intensity. He explained to Margarita:

"A path which has crossed an area of dense shade must suddenly come to an open, sunny area."

He planned to break the dense profusion of tropical trees and creepers, with areas of mown grass and almost suburban order. And he would contrast quiet atmospheres with the social busyness of his café.

Next he added elements which sharpened the sense of fantasy and stimulated his guests' imagination; a tower reached by a steep set of steps; a secret garden you could only reach by braving the formidable tunnel with its sense of dark creepiness; and a vine enclosed grotto. One final touch. To enhance the sense of a retreat from everyday life, he would screen all the boundaries, isolating the guests in his dream world.

By August 1932, José had completed most of the planned clearing and had laid out the paths and steps. He was ready to begin his main tree plantings. He had selected an area of open land which had been a grass pasture for cattle, before he purchased the property. He would plant here several thousand trees, mainly natives.

José was given expert advice by the Forestry Department. Fortunately his plans and theirs coincided. The Department contacted José.

"We want to ensure that representative stands of certain species are planted and nurtured. We are willing to supply the young trees on condition that you make every effort to ensure their survival and growth. These trees are never to be felled."

Forestry workers were sent to camp at Paronella Park to assist José with ground preparation and planting.

One section was planted with Hoop Pine, a species which grows naturally as a rainforest pioneer. It was particularly important for these trees to be cultivated, as natural generation is limited owing to the young seedlings' intolerance of shade.

The most dramatic planting was of an avenue of Kauri Pines. These grow naturally as a rainforest emergent but are particularly beautiful when given more room to develop. José and Margarita themselves established hundreds of other species, both native and exotic.

Finally they did extensive plantings of several varieties of bamboo, to act as a screen along the Park's boundaries and to add to the tropical character of Paronella Park.

Not content simply to plant and nurture the larger trees, José wanted to introduce more colour and variety to the understorey. When long term residents heard of his plans, they scoffed at his ideas. One elderly farmer came over personally to tell José:

"You'll be wasting your time. The rainforest soil is too poor to support ground cover. There isn't sufficient sunlight under the canopy."

As always when there was a challenge, José was determined to overcome the problems. The soil obviously needed enriching. He used a combination of natural mulches and manures and some chemical fertiliser. Then he contacted numerous nurseries and placed standing orders for any plant which would grow indoors or in the shade. He wrote to Government departments and to the Botanical Gardens. The local people became intrigued.

"You could try this creeper. My father used to grow it in full shade."

"This ornamental plant has lived in my lounge room for the last five years. I've taken some cuttings for you."

To help nurture young plants and propagate new ones, José built for Margarita a shaded orchid and fern house. Here she tended and watered, fertilised and staked, until the exotic plants were ready for transfer to the rainforest gardens. Some did not survive, but many flourished, against the odds.

The Botanical Gardens supplied Margarita with 50 varieties of Maidenhair ferns - to propagate and form the nucleus of a collection. She was delighted, not only to have the plants, but by the trust which professional horticulturalists placed in her ability.

But she never forgot that tropical gardening was always a new experience, with so many unknowns.

She was astounded by the speed of growth in the hot, moist conditions.

"Sometimes I stand very still - and then, I can actually hear the rainforest growing."

She found it hard to adjust to the incredible range of weather patterns.

"It's either the Big Wet or the Big Dry, and nothing much in between."

José and Margarita learnt to be flexible in their garden jobs, working with nature's seasons and weather.

Being in the grounds wasn't always hard work. They both shared a feeling of wonderment at the sheer beauty of the natural world around them. When walking early one morning along Teresa Creek, Margarita paused and putting her hand on José's arm, pointed to a spider's web, linking some tall trees. Drenched with dew, they looked like a curtain of frosty white gauze - the egg sacks, the pearl ornamentation on the filmy cloth.

They also loved to see the mist above the Falls, especially when it was sun- tipped, before the water fell to the silver river below.

Sometimes, however, their garden work brought them in touch with the other side of nature. Margarita was in the rainforest planting some ferns when she came upon a huge swarm of flies. Thinking something must have died, she went over to look. It took her eyes a moment to adjust to the shaded light. Then, she froze. A huge black python was shedding its skin. Giving one final frantic wriggle, the snake slid away into the undergrowth, less than a foot from Margarita's feet.

She crossed herself and left the flies to their feast.

By now, the gardens were taking shape. José had designed the pathways to form a hatch of intersecting walkways. He made them of compacted earth and sand, except in the upper gardens, where they were concreted. Many of the paths were bordered by balustraded fencing; the rest were marked with river stone edges and planted with ground ferns.

Water motifs ran throughout the grounds. The natural feature of Mena Creek Falls dominated. But this was simply an opening fanfare for the theme which continued in the narrower creeks and in the artesian spring which José had now named after his daughter Teresa.

To these natural water sources, José added several fountains, near the entrance and in front of the cafe.

As the visitor meandered along Teresa Creek, small bridges crossed and recrossed the stream, invitingly. At times, they served no real purpose other than 'The water is here, so let's cross it!' A kind of José's Folly.

One bridge, however, did have practical value. It gave access from the picnic area to Paronella Island, in the middle of Mena Creek. José had partially dammed the creek at this point to increase the flow under the bridge.

To add further interest, José constructed numerous pot stands, which lined walks, added focus to buildings and balustrades and once again, underlined the Moorish element.

These pot stands José made by using star pickets covered in concrete for the uprights. The pots he formed using barbed wire for reinforcing. Margarita would then plant up the completed pots with colourful flowers and trailing vines.

Finally, to display the true fairyland atmosphere of his Park, José strung electric lighting along the paths and buildings. The whole area was lit up and looked truly inviting. A perfect place for a romantic stroll after dinner.

Chapter Twelve

In the early 1930's, Mena Creek was a lively and growing settlement. It's people worked mainly in the sugar industry and in forestry.

The Paronella family were now very much part of this local community.

It was still a fairly isolated area with mill tramline and horses still providing the main transport. A train did run once a week to Innisfail but the journey took three hours. In parts, the line was so steep, the train sometimes had to back off and take another run at it. Or the passengers had to climb out and push and shove, if they wanted to reach their destination!

The roads were more like tracks. There was no bitumen. Some were covered in sand and gravel. The worst spots had tree trunks laid across them like corduroy. It made for a bumpy ride but at least you could get through.

In the hotel one day, a traveller was complaining about the muddy state of the local roads especially in the wet season.

"Bad roads mean good sugar land!" was the local response.

As early as 1920, a primary school had been established thanks to the efforts of Augustine Noone. He entered the names of his large family of children as potential pupils. In actual fact they lived in Innisfail, where they attended the local convent school. But the long list of names convinced the Education Department. The Mena Creek School building stood high on stumps. A wide shady verandah ran across the front and was much used, more often as shelter from the rain than the sun.

Both Teresa and Joe Paronella were pupils.

There were children from a wide range of backgrounds - Italian, Spanish, Greek, Maltese, Yugoslav, German, Chinese. They played together with an easy acceptance of their differences. Lunches were often exchanged - a salami sandwich for a peanut butter roll, a couple of falafels for a condensed milk sandwich.

Some children rode their bikes to school, others walked. At one stage José introduced a bus run, picking up along Utchee Creek and Donkin roads. He used an old flat tray truck on which he built a cage with wooden sides. A tarpaulin covered the top. The children were very fond of their 'monkey truck'.

A small group of tradespeople catered for Mena Creek's basic needs. John Themostoklys baked the most crusty bread and rolls, selling from his shop and also delivering by horseback. He would set off with a couple of hessian sacks full of bread slung over the horses back. Occasionally, a roll or two was bumped out and immediately swooped on by crows and currawongs.

There were a couple of general stores or you could have goods delivered from Silkwood. Jimmie Tate's store sold smallgoods, provisions, kero and farm produce. He used a more upmarket delivery method than the baker - the 'Push and Pull', an ingenious invention used to propel a small cart along the railway line. If a loco came, he had to unload, take it off the line and then, when the train had passed, reload and continue on his way.

Meat was delivered three times a week from Silkwood.

Social life was also catered for - by Noone's hotel. He called it Hotel Mena, after his daughter Philomena, who had also given her name to the village itself.

Noone employed six barmaids and they were kept flat out serving the thirsty customers. The hotel bar was noisy and full of activity; the dining room was more restrained and formal, with white cloths on the tables and silver cutlery.

Out front was a wide verandah, with hitching rails and a horse trough.

Noone had also built a community hall. There was as yet no church, so services were held in the hall whenever a priest could come out from Innisfail. The first ever service in the district had been at the old Bianci house in 1928. Reverend Father Bolger officiated, riding through torrential rain to reach the group of 18 parishioners.

Saturday night dances were held at the school. Everyone went. Babies slept beside the seats.

Monnie Gabasa recalls going to these dances with José', Margarita and Teresa.

"José would say: 'Come on, put on your best dress and I'll take you dancing.' We'd hurry to finish the dishes and feed Teresa. Then over to the school. There'd be an accordionist, even guitar or violin player. I loved the music. José and Margarita were very good dancers, very rhythmic.

Then there was supper. The men would light a fire out the back and boil water in a couple of old kero tins, for tea and coffee. And oh, the food! It was tremendous. Everyone bought a plate.

I was only a young girl. It was the highlight of my week."

Socialising also took place in the homes, with friends being willing to walk 10 miles or more, to spend a few hours in each other's company.

The children's free time was spent swimming or fishing. Mena Creek and the Falls was always a great attraction.

A rare treat was the visit from a travelling magician. He came with a horse and caravan and put on a great show.

"You didn't pay. He just passed the hat around. And we always brought some special goodies for his horse."

As you can imagine, José's building projects were attracting a lot of attention. Whilst parents only talked about his progress, the children went to take a look for themselves.

After school, two or three boys could always be found over at Paronella Park, pestering José with questions.

"Why are you plastering the outside of that building?"

"What do you need those pipes for?"

"Why can't we walk on that cement?"

José was very patient with them, often stopping work to explain some building technique. He only shooed them away if they interfered with the job's progress.

The construction programme had now reached José's largest, most ambitious building - the hall, which would act as ballroom, cinema, theatre and reception centre.

He had already planned the dimensions of this structure. He knew that his Tower would link to it, forming one total impression of Spanish design.

The exterior walls were again made from formed concrete, with stucco finish.

The corrugated iron roof was steep pitched and created a huge attic area. José roughly covered the attic floor with 4x4 fibro sheets, with planks forming a 6 foot wide boardwalk down the centre. This area proved too hot for anything other than storage. In fact, one day when an elderly helper was up there, he became overcome by the heat and fell through the plaster ceiling into the hall. Incredibly he wasn't badly hurt.

The interior walls of the hall were textured. José used two methods. He covered the wall in plaster and then pressed his hands on, in a swirling motion. He also used a special device - a spray gun which splattered the plaster at the walls.

On these walls, Margarita hung Spanish pictures and posters.

The furnishings were to be elaborate; blue velvet drapes edged in gold braid and fringing. These were used to cover the windows. For the stage, Margarita chose deep red curtaining.

José bought several hundred canvas seats for use when films were being shown.

For dances, the ballroom floor was shown in all its beauty - black bean timber in a parquetry design.

And from the centre of the ceiling hung José's pride and joy - a large revolving ball, specially made for him in America. It was constructed of 1270 mirrored facets, each hand cut and hand set in a large round globe. Coloured lights were set up in each corner of the hall, which, shining onto the mirrors, sent hundreds of shimmering spots dancing around the room.

The effect was magical and very romantic.

José in a relaxed moment, playing his guitar for Margarita

To enter the hall guests walked through the foyer. In this area there was also an icecream parlour, a café, kitchens, a bakery and a laundry.

Afternoon teas could now be served from here, with visitors seated in the loggia or outside on the terrace.

During the building of the hall, José had an accident, which came close to costing him one of his legs. He was working with some freshly poured concrete, when he fell and cut a gash in his left leg. Though deep and bleeding badly, Margarita bathed it and bandaged the wound. The bleeding eventually stopped and for a day or so, his leg seemed to be improving. Then it started to swell.

Margarita took him to the hospital. They kept José in for treatment but the swelling wouldn't go down.

The next day, the doctor called Margarita into his office.

"We're going to have to amputate. His leg is poisoned and it's passing into the rest of his body."

Margarita listened carefully to all his explanations.

Then she shook her head.

"No take his leg off. I take him home. I fix it."

And she did. Every hour she put a fresh poultice on the wound - alternating hot with cold. This she continued day and night until, one morning, she knew the swelling was easing. A few hours later, it had all gone.

José always carried a slight limp, but he had recovered from his ordeal, with leg intact, thanks to Margarita's refusal to give up.

The very last building which José constructed was, ironically, the only one which has crumbled without a trace. It was a gate house, situated at the entrance to the Park. From here, tickets would be sold and also souvenirs. By this time, José was running short of materials and did not make his usual strong mix of cement versus sand.

One of José's Spanish friends made a horseshoe shaped sign, from wrought iron, with Paronella Park written in flowing script. The design was pure Catalan, echoing the entrance to villas and palaces in Spain.

By 1935, all the major building work was completed. The total cost, in monetary terms, was in excess of £20,000. The labour and effort cannot be measured. Who can put a price on the fulfilment of a dream?

José's creation of Paronella Park was about to receive official recognition and praise.

A chamber of Commerce Conference was being held in Innisfail, with delegates from all over Queensland. As part of their itinerary, a visit was arranged to 'The Spanish Castle'.

In the group was the Governor of Queensland, Sir Leslie Orme Wilson. He was highly impressed both by José and his work. After enjoying one of Margarita's afternoon teas, Sir Leslie inspected the grounds with José. They were away a long time, apparently deep in conversation.

Later, the governor commented to journalists:

"José Paronella has created a place of beauty which will be a great attraction to visitors in the future. His buildings are of unique design. The Park is a credit to North Queensland. It is absolutely remarkable to see what one enterprising man can do."

José's Cottage and Castle

Lower Refreshment Rooms

Chapter Thirteen

The mining district of Mt Garnett lay 140 kilometres to the west of Innisfail. It was a bustling, rowdy place, with men coming from all over Australia, drawn by the hope of striking it rich.

In the early 1920's an Aboriginal woman took one of the miners as her lover. He was a European, one of the thousands working in the area. She was happy to be his woman and to look after the camp he had set up. And she was proud of the son she bore him. There was nothing unusual in the situation. It happened all the time. The men were lonely. The native women were available and willing. In these remote mining areas society's disapproval carried little weight. Sure, there might be some talk in Innisfail about Mario or Franco 'having a gin up there' - but who would ever know the truth?

A year or so earlier at Palm Island, off the Queensland coast, one of the aboriginal women gave birth to her son. The father was a man of her tribe. Because his mother was 'unmarried' in the eyes of the white authorities, the baby boy spent the first few years of his life in the special section established for unmarried aboriginal women and their children. At the age of 5 years, however, he was taken from his mother and was sent to live in the Boys Dormitory. This was to 'socialise the boys into new ways of thought and behaviour'. It was part of Government policy. The children were to be educated away from traditional tribal values and customs; away from the authority structure of their own people. The power which formerly went to the elder males of the tribe would now be given to the white administrators.

These two boys, the halfcast from Mount Garnet and the full-blood from Palm Island, by a series of circumstances, were to come together and share many years in each other's company. They would later be known as Jackie Cook and Albie Queensland.

Jackie's mother died of a fever when he was only a toddler. He was sent by his white father to be raised by the Cook family over at Nerada. After school, he went for a year to the Innisfail Rural School. There he learned woodwork and metalwork.

Once he was old enough to have a job, he was fostered to one of the local canefarmers, to help with all kinds of work on the farm. The name of his boss was José Paronella.

Albie had by this time been sent away to Palm Island to the South Johnstone area, under the Aboriginal Protection Scheme. He would be sent to work on one of the properties. His wages would be paid to the local police, who acted as Government agents. Albie would only be able to gain access to money by visiting the local police station. Aboriginals were not considered capable of managing their own affairs.

The farm Albie was assigned to was owned by José Paronella.

As employers go, Jackie and Albie could not have been more fortunate. José fed them well, provided them with adequate clothing and accommodation. And perhaps, more importantly, he trusted them and believed in their ability to take on responsibility - provided they were given clear instructions and guidance.

When José was well advanced with his building programme and tourists were beginning to visit, he decided to bring the two boys from the farm to live at Paronella Park. They were given a couple of rooms for sleeping, at the black of the garage. They became part of the family. Teresa later recalled: "They always sat at the kitchen table with Joe and I for all meals. And then, they'd help with the washing up.

José provided Jackie and Albie with work clothes and also with a set of good slacks and shirts for going into town or meeting guests. Both were extremely clean and tidy.

The two boys were vastly different in appearance. Albie was short, stocky and very strong. He had jet black hair, a wide nose and full lips.

Jackie was about 12 inches taller, thinner and more athletic looking. He had dark

Jackie and Albie

good looks, with warm brown eyes and an engaging smile.

In personality and temperament, they were also quite different.

Albie, from Palm Island, was quiet and serious. He sometimes had a far away look in his eyes, as though remembering some tribal legend or spirits.

Though the Paronella's treated him as one of the family, he always remained more of an 'outsider' than Jackie. Albie had many of the native Aboriginal ways of acting and thinking. His non-verbal behaviour, for example, carried the indirectness of facial expression and gesture common to his people. Whereas white men would point with hand and arm, Albie would gesture more subtly with eyes and lips. He would never walk or pass things across another person's path of movement or vision. He would go behind such lines.

And Albie never arrived or departed from social situations abruptly. Teresa recalls how he would approach slowly, even pausing - and always at an indirect angle from the group.

Albie's way of behaving was often misinterpreted as shyness.

José held Albie in very high regard.

"He is a hard worker. I leave him cutting long grass with a reaping hook. Some hours later, I come back. He is still working away steadily, and the job is almost finished."

Teresa recalls one peculiarity of Albie's.

"He loved anchovy toast. And he would dip it into his coffee. I'd say "Albie!'. He'd just smile and say "I like it."

In contrast to Albie, Jackie was outgoing and lively, with a strong sense of fun. He liked nothing better than being with children. He would tell them stories and chant nursery rhymes. When children came to the Park, they would go looking for Jackie. He had a kind of Pied Piper effect.

José smiled to himself one day, listening to Jackie, who was over in the meadow surrounded by children. He was singing with them in his slightly crackled voice:

"…the little boy laughed to see such fun
And the cow jumped over the moon…."

And at that point, Jackie threw his head back and let out his peculiar kookaburra-like laugh. The children were jumping up and down, joining in, imitating Jackie.

The same thing happened years later, when Jackie went over to one of the local farms to help with cane planting.

"He was on the drill there when we were putting the plants in. My sister's children were all there - must have been about eight of them. Jackie was telling them stories and they followed him along the furrow, single file - repeating everything he said. They couldn't leave him alone. They just loved his warm sense of fun."

José was gradually training Jackie and Albie. He soon felt that they were capable of doing more than just basic maintenance. They could be shown how to conduct tourists around the park.

José taught them the names of the various trees and plants. He showed them how to identify the birds and the exotic butterflies. Jackie was capable of even more responsibility so José showed him how to operate the film projection equipment in the cinema. To show his confidence in Jackie's ability, he was allowed to operate the equipment on a very important day. Once a year, the film distributors' agents came to the district to show the latest releases to all the cinema owners. They met at Paronella Park. Jackie acted as projectionist on these occasions. Not an easy task, when only sections of each film were being shown. José always introduced him politely to the visiting owners.

These two boys, Jackie and Albie, contributed thousands of hours of hard work towards making a success of the Paronella Park project. In return, the Paronella family gave them a home, a place to which they could belong.

And José felt a responsibility towards them. He often worried about their welfare. He knew the temptations that they faced.

One day Jackie went into Innisfail wearing an almost new shirt which Margarita had bought for him. He came home in a dirty, old, torn t-shirt.

Margarita was furious.

"We buy you good clothes. You lose them! It's not good!"

Jackie tried in vain to explain that he had met a group of town aborigines. They had taunted him about being half-white, saying: "You're not a real aborigine. You won't share your things with us. You want to keep them all for yourself."

Finally, Jackie couldn't take it any longer and he gave one of them his shirt.

José was also worried if they hung around the hotel. He tried to keep both of them from drinking alcohol. He felt he must protect them or they would suffer the fate of so many of their people - they wouldn't be able to handle the booze.

Would his worst fears be realised?

José and Margarita, with Albie and Jackie

Chapter Fourteen

Paronella Park provided a variety of activities to attract visitors. There was something to interest people of all ages.

Many older Innisfail residents recall driving out to the Park on a weekend afternoon. The drive itself was relaxing, passing through the lush green fields of cane. They strolled in past the gatehouse and cooled for a while in the shady patio area - perhaps enjoying a welcome cool drink.

Then they would descend the Grand Staircase and take a leisurely walk through the tropical grounds. They might spot unusual birds attracted by José's plantings; or marvel at exotic colourful butterflies.

Passing through the Tunnel of Love, visitors discovered Teresa Falls with it's miniature beauty - and the Secret Garden. Along the way they paused to listen to the crystal sound of the water tumbling onto the rocks; the breeze rustling in the rainforest canopy; a bush creature scuttling for cover.

In the distance could be heard the sounds of young people playing tennis or children romping in the meadow.

At last, afternoon tea beckoned and they made their way to the Café, and Margarita's fabulous home-made sponges; or scones and fresh cream. They sat on for quite a while, mesmerized by the beauty of their surroundings.

"We always drove away reluctantly but wonderfully relaxed."

For the younger people, there was the attraction of the water. There was easy access from the picnic area to the 70 metre diameter safe swimming hole. The water, coming down from the mountains through shady rainforest, was always cool and refreshing.

A diving board was provided but sometimes the more adventurous youths would swallow dive from the turbine tower, halfway up the Falls or even, occasionally, from the top of the Falls itself. This had dangers, as the diver had to clear the rocks which were at the base of the Falls.

Visitors enjoying the view of the falls

But - it was good fun and certainly caught the attention of the girls!

It was possible to swim in behind the curtain of water and clamber up onto the rocky ledge behind. On a hot Queensland day, this cool cavern area was very pleasant.

Those who chose not to swim, could borrow José's boat and row over to the Falls or back to the Island.

José had even fitted up lights so that guests could cool off with an evening swim.

Many of these young people would stay on to enjoy Margarita's dinner. There was no set menu. It was always Meal of the Day - most often chicken and spaghetti. The aroma from the kitchen was irresistible. The dining tables were set with red check cloths and the atmosphere was friendly and inviting.

For families with young children, Paronella Park provided the ideal picnic spot. It was totally safe for the children and adults could relax, while the children went exploring.

"We used to have a look first in the Museum. There was always something new since our last visit. I remember being fascinated by some old guns and imagining one of them pointed at me by a villain in a cowboy film. And there was a Spanish doll my sister always wanted to see. And a sailing boat trapped in a glass bottle. It was an endless source of interest."

"We used to play in the tunnel. It was very dark in there. You could just see the light at the far end. It was a great place to yell 'BOO' and frighten the girls."

"Then we'd go and poke the Conga eels. There were always some in the fountain. We used to bring crusts for them. One day we went to look but they had all gone. Mr Paronella said that they had nibbled some fresh concrete he was using to patch the pool and had died from concrete poisoning.

One day there was a great commotion. Some visiting Conga eels slid along the top of the Falls. Some people were watching as they cascaded down the waterfall into the pool below. Swimmers scattered in all directions. It was great fun!"

"I remember they had tame cassowaries and 2 wallabies. I'd never seen them close up like that before."

"We'd run down to the meadow where the slides and swings were set up. It seemed no time at all before Mum called us for lunch."

Lunch could be set up anywhere in the Park - but many visitors chose to use the picnic tables down by the water. It was cool and shady.

After lunch, while children continued exploring, parents took a welcome snooze.

"It was a magical place to us. We played all sorts of games, making up stories and acting them out as we went. We pretended there were monsters in the bush and made ourselves shivery with fright."

No visit to the Park was complete without an icecream, made by the Paronella family on the premises. José had bought a special machine, with two barrels, one inside the other. The gap between was filled with crushed ice and the inner barrel with milk and eggs. The mix was turned by a big handle, until it thickened. Homemade icecream from such pure ingredients was a delicious treat for adults and children alike.

At the end of the day at Paronella Park, the children went home taking vivid memories of this wonderland.

"Can we come again tomorrow?"

José's park was now truly the cultural and social centre for the Innisfail and South Johnstone community.

The tennis courts were installed and the Park became the venue for the local tennis club. On summer afternoons there was the sound of tennis balls being hit and many lightly dressed young players would be enjoying a leisurely game - with plenty of cool drinks afterwards on the Café terrace, as they watched the other matches.

The cinema operated once or twice a week. Before the main feature, José would show 5-6 minutes of his homemade movies, featuring the Park. Then the latest feature films would be screened. Seating was on canvas slung chairs and large fans whirred from the corners, keeping the humid air at least moving around.

Sometimes, there was more excitement in the cinema itself, than on the screen - especially when the show had to stop while José shot a couple of snakes. They had slithered in and coiled up beneath the seats, attracted by the soundtrack music.

The social highlight was the dances held in the Hall. A cover charge of 2 shillings, including supper. This was very good value. There was no alcohol. José himself would greet the guests on arrival and make them feel welcome. During the evening he would keep a close eye on the proceedings, making sure all was in order and everyone was having a good time.

The band was usually 4-5 musicians, many whom played by ear. They performed lively, rhythmic modern music.

José's revolving ball was a great success. All the main lights were put out. Showers of light fell on to the dancers, like coloured snow. It was very romantic.

"None of us young people ever missed a dance at Paronella Park."

José had yet another use planned for his Hall. In 1940, the first wedding reception was held.

The ballroom was so spacious it could cater for 400 or more guests. 80 foot long tables were set up down the length of the room. Covered in crisp white cloths, they were decorated with flowers and vines from the gardens.

José had ordered some special china from Gibson and Patterson, in England. It arrived just in time for the first wedding. It was a creamy white, with a picture of the Castle and of the Falls.

Streamers hung from the centre of the ceiling across the walls and the bridal table had a huge arch of flowers over it, with wedding bells.

Margarita was extremely concerned that such events should be a success. She attended to every detail.

Several local women were employed to help. They remember Margarita well.

"I loved working for her - but she was very strict. Everything had to be exactly right. She would stand at the end of a long table and check that all the cutlery was precisely in line."

"She inspected our uniform before we started work. Was our apron straight? Was our cap on correctly?"

"Mrs Paronella ruled with an iron fist. But - she was fair and approachable."

The main course served to the guests usually centred around chicken. Margarita cleaned and prepared the chooks in an open-fired copper, slow roasting them to a tasty perfection. As wedding bookings grew, Margarita talked the local baker into cooking the meat in his ovens for her.

After the meal and the speeches, guests gathered on the terrace overlooking the Falls. The grounds were lit with coloured lights. It was truly a fairytale setting.

José and Margarita made the ballroom available free for a major local event - the annual children's Ball. With the love of young people it delighted the Paronellas to be able to support the local school in this and other ways.

The Fancy Dress Ball was the highlight of the school year. All the children helped with the preparation of the ballroom. Whilst some put up strings of decorations, others worked on the dance floor.

"Preparing for it was as much fun as the event itself. We'd polish the floor. We'd get the cornsacks out, spread the sawdust that had kerosene mixed with it and we ran up and down the room."

Choosing and making the fancy dress caused great excitement. Some kept their costume a secret, others couldn't stop talking about their ballerina dress, clown outfit or snowman suit.

"One year, Barry Locke went dressed as a turkey."

"It was like a night of magic, with everyone transformed into something else."

José awarded prizes for the most original, the most imaginative costume. Then there was square dancing to a local band.

Diving board over the pool, alongside the picnic area

The mysterious entrance to the Tunnel of Love

The ballroom set up for a wedding

The Paronellas also made the Park available to the school for the Annual Sports Day. There was serious athletic events, as well as fun races such as the Egg and Spoon and the Sack race.

For the local children Paronella Park was a focal point, a source of immense interest and attraction; so much so that one local school rule read: No going over to Paronella Park during school hours.

One boy was in deep trouble when his mate kicked a football into the grounds.

"He sent me to retrieve it. I got caught. My punishment - 100 lines."

After school, it was a different matter. It was a favourite meeting place for a swim. When the hydro scheme was operating, the girls loved to put their feet out near the base of the plant in the turbulence of the bubbles.

"It was like a spa!"

Occasionally some of the more adventurous would dive from the top of the Falls.

"We would climb up there from rock to rock. It was a steep climb. It was frightening, standing there. You felt very tiny, looking down. We weren't supposed to be there. My mother didn't know I could swim, let alone do that. Once the teacher found out, we got into deep trouble."

One of the Koppen boys recalls going for a swim when there was a flood on.

"We were swimming below the Falls. Mr Paronella came down and chased us out. He thought we'd be drowned."

Koppen and his friends would often fish below the Falls, where the water became shallow and went over the rapids.

"We used to go down there with crusts of bread and let them float downstream. For sure, we would catch a black bream. Sometimes we came away with half a bag of fish!"

José welcomed visits from the children. Only occasionally did he become irritable or angry with them if they went too far in their pranks.

One of the boys recalls such an occasion.

"We dug up an ant's nest and rolled it down to see if it would go over Mena Creek Falls. It got stuck - and that night when the pictures were showing, the ant's nest got taken into the turbine and the power went out. Everyone knew it was us kids and we got the cuts. The girls, however, escaped punishment. We boys didn't think that was fair!"

José himself was now gaining immense pleasure from seeing the realisation of his dream. So many people were enjoying the Park and he felt a deep satisfaction. He loved to hear the comments of visitors and sometimes he would personally take a group of guests on a guided tour.

He enjoyed his image as a successful businessman; the entrepreneur who had developed this unique tourist park.

"I started with nothing. Hard work and more hard work. That's how it was done."

But José was more than just a businessman. He was a creative artist and Paronella Park was his monumental work of art. It displayed imaginative design, architectural planning and skilled craftsmanship.

Like any artist, José needed feedback. He wanted to show his creations to others and hear their response.

He was never more happy than when strolling through his Park chatting to visitors, explaining his concepts - the significance of design features; the technical problems he had struggled with; the setbacks; the successes.

Many visitors remember José in this role.

"He was so quiet and humble, yet so very proud of his creation."

Sometimes José would give detailed answers to questions, about the hydro scheme, or the problems of gardening under the rainforest canopy, or how he coped with slippage whilst digging the tunnel.

At other times he was less forthcoming.

"Mr Paronella. How many bags of cement did you use?"

With a shrug...."I no wish to count them!"

José would sometimes offer to row the visitors out to the Falls in his boat. Two or three ladies would eagerly climb aboard and José would take them out round the island and across to the cascading water. The spray would begin to shower the boat, causing the ladies concern about their dresses. José, always the gentleman, would produce a large umbrella.

José Paronella was now truly the host of a Spanish castle and Pleasure Grounds, to rival anything to be seen in Europe.

His work was admired. His dream was realised.

José loved to show his garden to visitors

The power of flood waters sweeping through the top gardens, 1994

Flood waters crash through José's ornamental ballustrades, 1994

José's Spanish Castle in the Top Gardens

Teresa Falls

Chapter Fifteen

A source of great joy to both José and Margarita was their friendship with other Spanish residents of the district. Though by no means as large as the Italian community, there were about thirty local Spanish families.

These fellow countrymen enjoyed social times together. They also provided a system of advice and financial backing. Business deals were sealed with a handshake over a glass of wine.

All shared a love of Spanish music and song. The families would come together for celebrations of birthdays, weddings and festivals.

José and Margarita always loved the party held to celebrate the 'cut out' - the completion of the cane harvest. This would take place at one of the farms, with tables set up outdoors. Huge dishes of pasta and risotto would be prepared, with bowls of salad and platters of the local fresh fruit. There would be plenty to drink with cases of Abbott's Lager and Bols Gin in stone bottles - and, of course, Spanish wine.

The women wore their prettiest cotton dresses; the men, slacks and open-necked shirt.

Conversation flowed freely, with news from home a favourite topic. It was also a good chance to catch up with local gossip. And newcomers would be introduced and made welcome.

There was always someone to play the accordion or strum a guitar. José himself loved to sing Catalan love songs. Long into the night, the plaintive music echoed through the cooling tropic air.

Christmas gave further cause for celebrations. Spanish friends would again gather on one of the farms, where a pig would be roasted on a spit. The next day they would visit another farm, and so on, until Christmas stretched into a two week long party.

Unfortunately, once Paronella Park was fully operational, José and Margarita could not join their friends at all the festivities. The Park was open for business over the holiday period.

The Spanish families also worked together in fundraising. When the Spanish Civil War broke out in July 1936, money was needed to support relatives and friends involved in

Spanish friends enjoying a social get-together

the hostilities. José and Margarita were particularly concerned as much of the fighting was taking place close to their relatives in Girona.

A Spanish Queen competition was held with money raised from dances and other social events. Seventeen year old Lily Garcia won both the Beauty Contest and the Queen of Fundraising award. She had raised £179.

Lily's family helped the cause in another, more direct way. Her father decided to go and fight against the Franco dictatorship.

He applied for leave of absence from the Goondi Mill and announced to his family: "I'm going off to Spain to fight with the International Brigade against Franco!"

At the end of his leave he came back and took up his job again, almost as though nothing had happened.

Lily Garcia was married soon after her father's return. She still treasures the wedding gift given to her by the Paronellas.

"It was a water jug and six glasses, made from pale green frosted glass, with bunches of grapes etched on the sides. It was a very generous gift for those days when money was so scarce."

The Donatui family were José and Margarita's closest friends. Claudio had come out to Australia from Girona and after establishing a basic home, sent for his family in 1913. The son, Joe, returned to Barcelona for a holiday and met and married Maria and brought her back with him.

Maria was very beautiful, very young and like Margarita before her, very inexperienced about Australian conditions.

The newly wed couple settled on Joe's farm. Joe immediately wanted to show off his new wife. He had already bought himself a car, a Buick which had belonged to one of the local solicitors. He also wanted to show this to his friends.

"Come on, Maria. Let's drive over to the Paronellas. You'll love Margarita. She'll be a good friend for you."

Maria was very concerned to do the right thing, to make a good impression.

She chose her best silk dress and wore a new pair of white shoes, with hat and gloves, of course. This is how they went visiting in Barcelona. It had been raining overnight and the roads were slushy. But Joe drove carefully and all went well - until they came to a very muddy section and the car bogged.

"It's OK" Joe reassured the worried Maria. "I've got some planks in the back. We'll soon be out of this. Hop out and give me a hand."

Maria hesitiated - but she was very young and he was her new husband. She did as he said.

Half an hour later, the Donatuis arrived at the Paronella farm.

Margarita took Maria aside to help her clean up. The silk dress was ruined. There was no way the sticky red mud could be removed. Maria was in tears.

José with his Spanish friends, Salvio and Benito Salleras

The next time Maria went to Innisfail she went along to See Poy's store. A Spanish lady was fortunately there to interpret Maria's urgent request.

"I want some dresses which wash, which can be thrown in the copper, which mud comes off!"

Years later when the Paronellas were visiting the Donatui family, the women were reminiscing.

Maria smiled. "You know, I still have some of those cotton frocks from See Poys. They must have been washed a hundred times!"

José and Margarita's Spanish background was strongly felt in every aspect of their family life. José was absolute Head of the Household. Margarita deferred to him for everything. Only occasionally would she grumble afterwards to Teresa.

Her daughter showed little sympathy.

"I don't know why you won't stand up to dad. Tell him if you don't agree with him!"

But Margarita took her wifely role very seriously.

"No. A woman must support her husband, even when he is wrong."

Young Joe, in temperament, was very like his mother. He would do as he was told, rather than risk arguments and trouble.

Teresa was quite different, and far more like José. She was volatile and quick-tempered. At times, she would challenge her father's authority and heated arguments would result. But the hostilities didn't last long, for underneath, there was a deep bond of love and respect between father and daughter.

Both were intense and dramatic, expressing extremes of emotion. José hardly ever sat still. His energy always needed expression in movement. Even when talking to Margarita, he would stand up to explain some idea, walking up and down, demonstrating with his hands.

To be relaxed, José had to be absorbed in activity, whether building or gardening or - working on his cars.

For some reason, José's car always seemed to have problems.

"The ute needs fixing," José would tell Margarita. And he would disappear to the garage for hours on end.

Margarita would say, "I've never seen anyone like your dad for cars. He knows so much about them - he can repair them without a mechanic."

Teresa was more critical.

"Dad just likes messing around with machinery."

Despite the work he did servicing his vehicles, José was often plagued by breakdowns and accidents. In most cases, these were the result of the appalling condition of the unmade roads.

His most serious accident happened when he had been working at his mine. He was on his way back, looking forward to a relaxing meal and a good sleep. He was coming down a steep hill. There was a sickening noise from under the car and José was losing control. The axle had smashed into a

Teresa with José at the Innisfail Show

The Paronella family, José, Teresa, Baby Joe and Margarita - with one of José's favourite cars

rock and was broken. José had two choices. Risk the car running over the edge into the steep gorge - or run it into a tree. He chose the latter. The impact pinned José under the steering wheel. He had survived but with several broken ribs.

"It wasn't the car's fault!" was his only comment to Margarita.

From a very early age both the Paronella children were needed to help with the Park activities. They accepted this as a natural part of family life. Joe only really complained once and that was when he was called out from school when some unexpected visitors arrived at the Park and his mother needed him to show them around.

Teresa and Joe attended the local Mena Creek School. They would run home together, anxious to be free of classroom restriction. Margarita would be waiting for them, with a drink and a bun or a cake. Homework was minimal and was soon completed. But then it was time to do their chores.

"Joe would help rake the paths, hose down the picnic tables, brush the patio. My jobs were in the house - especially helping with the laundry. Mum would wash the linen in a copper, adding soap and a bit of kero. The water was beautifully soft. The sheets and tablecloths were hung out in the top paddock to dry. It was my job to bring them in and fold them ready for ironing. And cleaning shoes! That was my responsibility. Mould grew on everything. So once a week I took everybody's shoes out into the porch and cleaned and aired them."

After dinner, if the weather was fine, the children would extend the day as long as possible. They would ride their bikes, or play with the dogs. Blackie belonged to Joe, Titus to Teresa.

Once inside they would settle in the lounge. Teresa was learning the piano, so she would practise her pieces. But other activities were limited.

"There weren't many books in our house. Dad didn't like us reading. You didn't sit down to read a book. Oh no. Dad thought that was lazy."

"Can't you find some sewing to do?" he would ask.

Their main entertainment came from the radio, a large floor-standing console model.

"We listened to the news, and music - and all the serials. Sometimes we had to turn the volume up real loud, to hear it over the sound of the Falls."

School holidays brought great freedom.

"We used to go fishing from the bank of the creek. Joe loved it. There were thousands of catfish in there. Mum liked eating them, so we always caught her a few."

And they went swimming, usually with Jackie and Albie.

"And dad would take Joe and I out for days in the car. Mum never came. She always had too much to do. We'd go to the Malanda Jungle tourist park and watch aborigines climbing trees and doing corroboree dances. Or to the tablelands to see the butterflies. And sometimes Dad took us to the mine at Herberton and we'd stay overnight in a boarding house. That was a special treat."

The children had a good relationship with their parents and were involved in the practical day to day activities and work of the Park. Despite this and even as they grew older, they were never included in business discussions. These took place strictly between José and Margarita. Teresa and Joe would be sent away.

"We only knew a very little about Dad's business plans. Just what Mum was willing to tell us."

But, all in all, it was a childhood which Teresa recalls with pleasure.

"We wanted for nothing. We had a lot of good times. Mum spoiled us a bit and though Dad was sterner, he was very fair."

The Paronella family

Café in José's Castle

Café in the Top Gardens

Chapter Sixteen

José had problems.

Paronella Park was not proving to be a financial success. It was in fact, barely breaking even. José's dream was not standing up to the harsh realities of profit and loss. It was the worst business investment he had made.

Over the years of building, José had spent at least £20,000, in order to set up his Park as a going concern.

Now when he would have anticipated reaping good earnings, the outgoings were so high that there was no profit from the venture. And this was despite all the hard work and effort of his family and their two aboriginal helpers, Albie and Jackie.

In the creation of his dream, José had overlooked two commercial factors: the cost of upkeep and the present state of the tourist market.

The amount of work needed to keep the buildings in good order and the grounds maintained was never-ending.

The climate was always working against José's venture. The concrete work soon showed signs of mould and mildew and had to be cleaned regularly. José decided that the main buildings would have to be whitewashed but this in itself was a time-consuming job. Periodic floods would wash away ballustradings or damage the picnic tables. Rainforest creepers threatened to take over any man-made structure and needed constant trimming.

Having his Park on two distinct levels added considerably to the work load. So much had to be carried up and down, including all the provisions for the Café by the Pool.

The whole enterprise was becoming highly labour intensive.

Despite all the family help, staff were still needed and had to be paid. The tourist industry in Northern Queensland was in its infancy. It had been held back in the Thirties by the Depression. Even those people with jobs considered carefully before spending money on luxuries such as holidays.

Though Paronella Park was proving immensely popular with the locals, interstate tourists were few and far between. And only one company, the White Car coaches, was bringing Brisbane people to the area. Their itinerary included a visit to the 'Spanish Castle'.

José was ahead of his time. The concept of his tourist park was indeed wonderful for the hundreds who came to enjoy it. But the costly upkeep needed thousands coming through the turnstiles.

Teresa said later: "It was a hard road to hoe to make money."

It was up to José's other business activities to keep the family's finances in the black. Fortunately, José believed in diversity in his investments and enterprises.

Money was still coming in from tin mining. José now owned an alluvial mine at Hot Springs near Ravenshoe. The mined tin was washed and then sold for cash in Herberton.

In the early days, José had, unbelievably, ridden his bike to the mine. One day, he had a puncture but was fortunately picked up by Mr Alister, who had a garage business in Ravenshoe.

By the late 1930's, José had a utility and then a truck. He would spend several days at a time up there and return at the weekend with enough money to continue his Park operations. He would always leave two or three aboriginal boys working there in his absence.

Margarita hated José's trips to the mine. The road was still treacherous and if her husband was late back, she would phone the police.

"Has Mr Paronella passed by? Have there been any accidents?"

José held onto the mine until the early 1940's, when he sold it for £400.

José's other investments were still profitable, including repayments he was receiving on loans made over the years. And he was still involved in buying and selling farms.

José's versatility, even in small projects, sometimes made Margarita smile.

"I have a new plan," he announced seriously one morning. "I am renting some land to grow bananas. We will sell them at the Park."

And they did - at two for a penny!

José's shrewdness resulted in another source of revenue. He installed two petrol bowsers. These were operated manually by pumps. During the Thirties, quite a few motor cars were coming into the district. The farmers also needed petrol for the new machinery and as they didn't have tanks on their farms, they came to Paronella Park in their utes and filled drums. The profit margin on petrol sales wasn't very high but it was constant.

The Paronella family's overall finances were still floating and growing. After having made money, José was extremely careful to protect and consolidate his funds. He did his own weekly totals, using a professional accountant only for tax purposes.

José had a strong aversion to banks. In the early years, he was able to operate on a completely cash basis. He paid for his land in cash; for staff wages and for all provisions and equipment needed on his farms.

He had opened only one bank account for use when he was overseas. Even José knew that he could hardly leave large amounts of money lying around during his absence. He seldom used this account until he began to rent films for his cinema. The film distributors were very hard in their dealings. Cinemas were being set up in community halls all over the state. To ensure that they received their payments, films shown over the weekend had to be paid for on Monday, by cheque.

José would keep the amount in balance in his account low, just enough to cover the movie fees.

Many men in José's position, handling large amounts of cash, couldn't resist the temptation to gamble. Not José! He never gambled. The closest he ever came was when one of his friends called in one day to tell José about a horse that was 'an absolute certainty!"

"You can make a fortune! Today!"

José hesitated - then took £200 from his pocket - and then he put it back again.

"I make it. I keep it."

Those who did business with José regarded him as straight forward and honest, but as a tough businessman and a shrewd, hard dealer.

He was always on the lookout for trading opportunities. He would make careful purchases of farms, where the owners were strapped for cash through over-reaching. He would buy, improve and re-sell, often taking the finance himself.

José was single-minded in the pursuit of profit. Even friends and neighbours didn't stand in the way of business. The Noone family of Mena Creek had known the Paronellas for years. Yet, when their hotel lease came up for renewal José apposed it. He believed the hotel was bringing too much competition, especially for weddings, the Licensing Board overruled his objection. The Noones were very upset, but José saw his action as normal business practice.

To his workers, José was always Mr Paronella, the boss. He expected dedication to the job; in turn, he looked after his staff well.

Whilst José and Margarita went on a rare holiday to Melbourne, José employed Spanish friends, the Gill family, to manage the

José in middle age

Park. Frank, their son, was only seven at the time.

"Dad and Mum had to work hard for Mr Paronella. But he was always very good to our family."

The Gill caretaking began badly.

"The first week after the Paronella's went away, the projectors broke down in the picture theatre. I remember Mum saying 'Wouldn't you know! They've only just left and this had to happen!'

The Gill family slept in an area of the tower, over the kitchens. Frank shared a room with his baby brother. One night, Frank woke to see a snake crawling along the wall. It had been attracted by the warm milk in the baby's bottle.

"I yelled for Mum as I'd never yelled before!"

Frank has fonder memories of the rest of his stay.

"I sometimes used to go with Albie and Jackie as they showed visitors around. I learnt the patter from them and could have done it myself, except that at 7 years I was a bit young to act as a guide."

José and Margarita returned in due course. Margarita especially was very glad to be home and take up the regular routine of life at the Park.

José was always restless for new challenges. He was an opportunist, constantly considering possible new enterprises.

"You know those cable cars we saw in Europe? I reckon I could construct one at Gordonvale, to take people up to the top of the 'Pyramid'. We could build a restaurant up there."

And at the Park itself, he was always experimenting with growing plants that could be turned into a commercial crop. First it was ginger and then watercress and then - mushrooms. He knew quite a lot about their culture and varieties as his native Catalonia had a wonderful reputation for mushroom growing.

"We could try them in the tunnel!" he told a sceptical Margarita.

Though many of his ideas never developed into full-blown schemes, his mind was

Back row, L to R: Albie, Teresa, Mrs Gill, Jackie, schoolteacher Colin Bevan.
At front: Joe and Frank Gill

always active, always thinking and planning, always evaluating.

His business acumen was sound - with the exception of his major venture - his dream, his beloved Paronella Park.

Gun collection in José's Museum

Entrance to the Ballroom

Chapter Seventeen

When war broke out in Europe in 1939 Australia was inevitably bound up in the hostilities. Recruitments and troop movements were soon to make an impact in the capital cities.

The South Johnstone Shire, however, seemed a very long way from the action. True, fundraising committees were formed and 'Send Offs' were organised for the local boys who had signed up. News of events in Europe was keenly followed on the radio.

Yet there was a sense of 'It's happening to them, not us.'

But all this was to change. With the Japanese attack on Pearl Harbour the war was suddenly very close. On 7th December 1941, 360 carrier-born aircraft, launched from a position 200 miles north of Hawaii, attacked the Pearl Harbour Naval Base. In just two hours, three quarters of USA air strength and one third of the army's planes were destroyed. And in the harbour, 5 battleships and 3 destroyers were sunk or damaged beyond repair.

Australia's long-held fear of invasion from the North seemed likely to become a reality. Foreign policy underwent a dramatic revision. Instead of helping Britain in a foreign war, Australia needed to defend herself and to find support from a powerful ally in the Pacific region.

Prime Minister Curtin's words were broadcast to a stunned nation: "I make it quite clear that Australia looks to America, free of any pangs as to our traditional links or kinship with the United Kingdom."

The effect of these events on the Innisfail region was immediate. The relaxed early days of the war were over. Special wartime rules were made. Some of these related to the large number of Italians in the district, many of whom had never taken Australian citizenship. They were technically Italian citizens. Whilst previously this had been ignored, now, many of them would be interned. The first group of internees left Innisfail in February 1942. It wasn't just the Italian families who were traumatised by this. The whole community was affected. Everyone had Italian friends or workmates. For years they had contributed to the local region. Suddenly they were part of the enemy. It raised uncertainty and confusion in people's minds.

Meanwhile the Japanese armies had moves rapidly southwards. When Hong Kong fell, headlines in Australia announced: 'He's coming South'

On 8th February, Singapore, defending itself from attacks from the sea, was taken by a Japanese force which came overland, having entered from the north west coast of the island.

This opened up all of Southern Asia to Japanese attack, leaving Australia totally exposed.

Australia recalled her troops from Europe and the Middle East.

At dawn on 19th February, 54 Japanese bombers and 27 fighter aircraft attacked Darwin. Eight ships were lost, 24 aircraft destroyed and 138 people killed.

The first reaction of the Australian public was shock.

Australia suddenly seemed very alone and unprotected.

By 8th March, the Japanese had occupied Rabaul, Lae and Salamaua in New Guinea. Australia's situation was desperate.

America, having lost its bases in the Philippines, decided that the only course of action was to regroup its airforce in Australia.

In April 1942 General Douglas MacArthur arrived to conduct operations in the region.

North Queensland became a hive of military activity.

In the South Johnstone area, many women and children had already been evacuated. The remaining population were told very little about the military situation. 'The less they know, the better' seemed to be the government's policy. But this left so much worry and concern.

People began to take their own precautions. At the schools, teachers kept drums of water on the verandah in case of fire after bombing raids. The children were required to have 'camouflage capes'. Many of the mothers made these from sugar bags, painted with green vegetation. The children also wore identity discs.

Air raid shelters were built.

José had refused to allow his children or wife to be evacuated.

"We will stay together" was his policy.

He did, however, construct an air raid shelter underneath the shed in the carpark. He dug a deep trench and timbered the sides to stop the red clay from falling. He put a can toilet at one end, screened by a hessian cover. Shelves were attached to the walls, to store food, candles, lamps and blankets. The whole shelter was underground and reached through a trap door.

For those days it was an elaborate structure. Most people just dug a hole and threw some sheets of corrugated iron over the top.

As tensions grew the government gave the remaining population little consolation or reassurance. They were left in no doubt that, in the event of an invasion, the army would not be able to help them. It would be too busy repelling the enemy. They would have to fend for themselves. "Head for the hills" was the only positive advice. And escape routes were indeed planned to the Western mountains.

With so many of the population gone, through enlistment, evacuation and internment, there was a severe shortage of labour. Basic food was rationed; tyres and spare parts were hard to come by and fertiliser was in short supply.

American forces were gathering in Queensland to drive the Japanese back. In April 1943, 111,000 USA troops were serving in the S.W. Pacific. By December of that year, there were half a million.

The significance of the American presence was felt dramatically in the whole Cairns/Innisfail area. The troops brought a kind of determination and assurance with them. Confidence was lifted. The incredible resources of the American forces and their unbelievable organization staggered the Australians.

The significance of the American presence for José Paronella was that, almost overnight, it brought prosperity to his ailing venture.

Paronella Park was in the ideal location to take advantage of the need for R&R - for both the American and Australian forces. Thousands of servicemen were now stationed in Cairns and throughout the Atherton Tablelands.

The carpark was soon full of military vehicles. The free-spending Yanks, with their Cairns and Innisfail girlfriends, were desperate for a respite from the war, for some normality; a swim, a stroll through the grounds, a meal, a dance.

To war-weary servicemen Paronella Park seemed like a mirage, a dream Spanish Castle and Gardens growing so incongruously from the tropical vegetation. So beautiful, so unusual, so fascinating - and so peaceful.

They relished it all.

A cool swim was welcome after the hot drive to Mena Creek. There was a lot of banter and joking. Some of the Americans would always show off to their girls by bravura swallow dives from the top of the Falls.

Sometimes they would throw a baseball into the water and when one of the local kids retrieved it, he was awarded with a handful of silver change from the men's pockets. They really had no idea of what Australian money was worth.

Jackie earned himself good pocket money in an unexpected way. He had, naturally, a very unusual laugh. With his warm, outgoing nature, it was often heard ringing through the gardens. It was not unlike a kookaburra. When Jackie realised how much this amused the Americans he played it up. They would pay him 5 shillings, a generous amount in those days, to hear him laugh.

Later in the day the men and their girls would enjoy a romantic walk through the Tunnel and along Teresa Creek - the men in their handsome service uniforms, the girls in bright summer dresses.

"It was like something from another world," wrote one Yank. "I met my wife in Innisfail and proposed to her in the Tunnel of Love. She accepted by the time we reached the other end! I'll never forget that day."

There was great demand for afternoon teas and for the evening meal which Margarita prepared.

"All you could eat for 4 shillings."

Seventy American servicemen came over every Sunday from their camp near Gordonvale. So many visitors stayed for dinner that Teresa recalls the huge trays in which they prepared Paella- Spanish rice. Though many supplies were short, Margarita was able to use produce from their garden. Homegrown tomatoes and herbs flavoured the food.

One of the few occasions when José lost his temper with a guest occurred over criticism of Margarita's cooking.

An American serviceman made the comment that the pasta sauce he had been served wasn't good as they made it 'back home'.

José grabbed him by the arm and pulled him out to the kitchen.

"See! That's what goes in the sauce - fresh tomatoes, fresh herbs, basil, oregano, garlic. What more do you want?"

The poor airman was profuse in his apologies.

"I guess I was just yearning for my Ma's home cookin'."

After the meal, there would be calls for Teresa, now an attractive teenager.

"Where's the young Spanish lady with lovely brown eyes?"

They wanted her to play the piano. Teresa loved these sessions. She'd play the latest hits and the Yanks would sing along.

"They wanted to tip me, but I said 'No'. My father is the owner. You are our guests.' So they passed a hat around to buy the music for songs I didn't have."

Some evenings there was dancing or films. The last cars didn't leave the carpark until the early hours of the morning.

On the whole the relationship between the American and Australian servicemen was friendly. Only occasionally did problems arise over competition for the local girls. The Yanks were then seen as a threat.

At other times, the Australians profited. Innisfail was a mecca for servicemen wanting sex. The brothels were so busy that the men had to queue. Australians short of cash for beer would join a queue and later quite happily sell their place to an American.

It wasn't only the brothels who profited from the American presence. There was a business bonanza in general. For Paronella Park, these were to be the boom years. José was reassured that he was now financially successful with his dream castle and park.

Though the largest profits came from the Americans, the Park was to be remembered long after the war by many of the Aussie soldiers.

Bruce Downie was an 18 year old when he made his one visit to Paronella Park. Like so many Australian servicemen, he was inexperienced and untravelled when he joined up. They were excited to be going interstate on a troop train, at seeing Sydney for the first time.

"We were country boys. We didn't know a bee from a bull's foot."

They reached Townsville.

"It was a buzz - alive with troops of all descriptions."

Finally, he was posted to Cairns; to the camp they called "The Sheridan Street Swamp".

Even now, all these years later, Bruce still has vivid recollections.

"Every so many days we would be allowed a day off. But because the area was under military rule, we were only allowed to travel in a limited radius. My mate and I took the Tin Hare train to Innisfail. It was a funny old thing - a single carriage with a diesel motor at the front. But when you've been stuck in one place for weeks on end, a Tin Hare looks like a Mercedes 500 coupe!

We then hitched a ride out to Mena Creek. It was still early in the day and not many other visitors had arrived. We wandered about the gardens. It was so peaceful we didn't even speak to each other. We saw the Falls from an opening down below, a sort of downstairs balcony. It gave a wonderful feeling as you stood and listened to the rush of the water going past. When we heard the story about the turbo, we marvelled at the genius who could think of harnessing this water, which never seemed to stop.

We went for a swim and then sat by the creek watching the fish jump. To my mate and I it was a very special day. I suppose we would now know that we were responding to the beauty of nature, gently controlled and moulded to create an atmosphere of pure enchantment.

It was half a century ago. We were boys who were deeply affected by everything we saw. It isn't the same today.

As the world changed at the end of the War and we all travelled - someone threw some shrinking liquid over all the magic. But I will always be glad that for that one day, José Paronella showed me that dreams can be fulfilled and hopes brought to fruition.

"Thank you, José"

1946 Flood

Chapter Eighteen

José and Margarita were listening to the radio when the announcement came through. On 15th August 1945 the Japanese had surrendered.

The 100,000 troops stationed in the area would almost immediately begin to go home. Life would return to normal.

"But things will not be the same," predicted José.

The first change to emerge was one which, fortunately for the Paronella's, would bring continued prosperity to Paronella Park.

Interstate tourism had been at a virtual standstill during the war. With peace came a surge of interest in trips to the North. Tourism started to boom. Some of these visitors were people who used to holiday in Queensland before the war - but thousands of new customers came, seeking a unique, different quality in their holiday destination or for warmer weather during the cold southern winters.

The Cairns/Innisfail area was certainly able to offer the climate - and some unusual trips; to the Great Barrier Reef, the off-shore islands, the cane fields and mills, the tea plantations and to the Spanish Castle.

Added to the interstate visitors were the increasing numbers of local people who now owned a car. Many had learned to drive whilst in the forces and there were a lot more cars on the roads. "We should be able to keep the Park running at a profit," José reassured Margarita.

Despite the sound state of his finances, José was beginning to have moments of worry; of ill-defined apprehension. He could not put his finger on the cause.

At night when Teresa and Joe were in bed, Margarita would sometimes stay up knitting or sewing. José would sit outside in the porch and think about the future.

He knew that already the population of South Johnstone was beginning to decline. In the wartime, the shortage of workers had pushed many farmers and other businesses into developing machinery to compensate for lack of manual labour. This trend would continue. José could see the time coming when places like Mena Creek would become rural ghost towns.

He worried about this. And he worried about his family, especially young Joe. He was now in his early teens and it had been José's decision to send him to school in Brisbane, to Nudgee College. He was determined that his son have what he himself missed out on - an education at a first class school and then, maybe, even at university. Joe might study business or accountancy and would be well-prepared to take over José's business interests and keep the dream alive. Yet Joe didn't seem interested in his studies.

And Teresa. She had a boyfriend - Aldo. José was not happy about this. Aldo had met the Americans during the war and heard about their country and the good lifestyle. He already had a brother in the States and wanted to go and live there. José didn't want Teresa to leave Paronella Park, let alone Australia. When Teresa married, his son-in-law should join the family and help with the running of the Park. He told Teresa: "Wait and see how he gets on in America."

José thought about taking a break and making another trip to Europe. He sometimes

José, Joe and friend

found himself becoming tired suddenly. He put it down to the long hours of work during the prosperous war years.

"We need a holiday, but we can't take it just yet."

José, for the first time in his life, did not feel optimistic about the future. Vague doubts and uneasiness continued to disturb him.

Soon he had to acknowledge that it was more than family or business worries.

He was beginning to notice symptoms of physical illness. He was having difficulty with digesting his food. He often had heartburn or indigestion. Sometimes he would even vomit his meal back up.

By late 1945, he could no longer conceal his symptoms from Margarita. She insisted he seek medical advice. At first José refused.

"I'm not ill," he shouted. "I don't need a doctor."

Eventually, Margarita prevailed and José went to Innisfail to see their family physician.

He gave José a thorough examination, asked lots of questions. He wanted José to see a specialist in Brisbane in the New Year. José was uncooperative. A compromise was reached. The doctor gave José some medicine to help ease the sickness. If the symptoms became worse, he was to return for a referral to a specialist.

That evening José again sat outside in the cool air. It was quiet, except for the sound of the Falls and the call of an occasional night bird. He looked across at his castle tower. He thought about all he had built. Suddenly it didn't comfort him as it had in the past. He felt a sense of separation, a sense of imminent disaster. He heard a faint rumble of thunder, the beginnings of a tropical storm.

He stood up and went back inside to be with Margarita.

The Tennis Courts at Paronella Park

José's Theatre

Chapter Ninteen

In February, the new school year began. José decided to go down to Brisbane with Joe and take the opportunity to do some errands.

Leaving his son at Nudgee College he made his way into the centre of town.

He had some paperwork to do at a government department. They kept him waiting around a long time and José was becoming irritable and tired. Finally the clerk gave him the completed papers and he walked towards the main shopping centre.

Without any apparent warning, José became dizzy and collapsed. By a strange coincidence some friends from Innisfail were also in Brisbane that day. They saw José fall down and ran across the traffic to help him. He was struggling to get to his feet.

"We'd better take you to the hospital".

José refused.

"I can't stay in Brisbane. I must get back to Mena Creek. I'll be alright in a minute."

Sitting in the train on the long trip back north, José felt a wave of incredible sadness sweep over him - and a deep sense of impending disaster.

He tried to reason himself out of it. He thought about his family and his beautiful Park - all the buildings and grounds just as he had imagined them, all those years ago. At least he had created something lasting, a heritage for his children.

The weather round Innisfail had closed in and heavy rain was falling. José only just made it home before the creeks and rivers rose, closing off the roads and railway line.

Margarita and Teresa were so relieved to have him safely home. He decided not to mention his illness.

He told himself: 'It's not worth worrying them. It was nothing. I'm fine now.'

Putting on a raincoat and gumboots he went to check the Park. The Hydro Electric scheme was functioning smoothly. He knew there wouldn't be any visitors in this kind of weather so he closed up the Café and Pavilion, checked there was no rubbish building up in the tunnel and carefully put away all the tools and equipment.

"It'll be a few days before these will be needed again, he thought to himself."

What José did not know was that an incredible set of circumstances were coming together. All his vague fears of disaster were to come tragically true.

A tropical cyclone had formed in the Coral Sea. The south east winds picked up the moisture and moved it onto the Queensland coast. The intense rain depression brought widespread tropical rain to the whole region.

José was frustrated at not being able to do any work, and the loss of income with no visitors. The rain, was just a part of life - a consequence of living in the wettest region in Australia. The yearly average was 148 inches.

When José had first come to live here one of the locals had warned him:

"Floods are nothing unusual. The North and South Johnstone Rivers meet at Innisfail and go out to sea at Flying Fish Point. If there's a king tide, then it banks all that water up. Combine this with exceptional rain in the Tablelands, the source of the rivers, and we've got floods - all over the region. You have to just learn to live with them."

There were always some indoor jobs to do. José, Jackie and Albie were finishing some painting work in the Ballroom; Margarita and Teresa were polishing glasses in the Hall kitchen.

"Thought you said we wouldn't have any visitors today," Teresa called out to her father as a truck pulled up in the carpark.

It was one of the local farmers, Herbie Dunn.

He had managed to drive through the flooded roads to reach them. He brought some terrible news.

A dangerous situation had developed upstream. Loggers had been working to cut the last of the giant cedars in the creek's catchment area. A large number of the felled trees, trimmed and ready for transport to the timber mill, were piled up on the low ground near the creek.

"The rising flood waters have lifted some of the logs into the stream. They are heading for the railway bridge!"

The implication of this news was devastating. José knew that flood waters carrying even the odd uprooted tree could damage man-made structures and turn them into splinters. He'd heard stories of the 1913 flood when the reinforced concrete Daradgee Bridge over the North Johnstone River was destroyed. The roaring cascades of water had torn the concrete pylons out of the river bed and twisted the bridge over.

José's mind filled with the awful possibility.

In that drama-charged moment, something happened which sent a chill through José's whole being.

Before his eyes he saw the level of water coming over the Falls drop suddenly. Within minutes, there was only a trickle - and then, absolute silence. For the first time since José had known the Falls, no water fell.

There was only one explanation. The logs had jammed against the railway bridge, creating a dam. Within the hour, a vast lake had formed. In the rising waters, more and more debris and logs were picked up and added to the pressure on the bridge structure.

The crackling roar of the bridge collapsing echoed sickeningly across the paddocks.

A fifty foot wall of water, carrying the huge cedar logs, was now heading directly for Paronella Park.

A rare photo, taken as the flood poured through the Castle, 1946

José's neighbours tried desperately to help; to drag the logs from the water. But it was hopeless.

Nature was in control and no man could stop her.

The Falls had been eerily silent for an hour or more. Not even a ripple. Then José heard the sound of the raging waters in the distance. He watched helplessly as the torrent, carrying its cedar rams, converged on his dream Park.

A local farmer who had tried to help, described the waters as a stormy sea, tossing six foot diameter logs around like matchsticks.

"The force was totally unbelievable. It was a power I've never seen before or since. Frightening. Appalling."

Concrete balustrades were picked up and thrown into the air; masonry tables uprooted from the ground. The Café and Pavilion were rapidly covered in water - doors pushed open by the force, logs smashing windows, furniture, the piano - anything that came in their way.

José yelled above the sound of the raging waters: "It's no use! We'll have to get back to the cottage."

He had almost left it too late. The waters were swirling with incredible strength. Teresa recalls the drag of the water against her dress. They clung to each other and desperately fought the current just making it back to the higher ground of the cottage.

The dogs were barking to them from the hill at the back of the house.

Teresa recalls a feeling of unreality.

"It was like we were watching a film. There was a sense of detachment. This wasn't really happening!"

The flood waters covered the upper gardens, rose to window level in the Hall, sending cedar logs crashing through into the foyer, the kitchen, the ballroom. One log tore a huge hole in the western wall. A section of the ballroom parquetry floor caved in.

The local paper was to report:

'Steel girders were snapped like splinters as the logs smashed down the concrete handrails and removed whole flights of steps.

Another log shot over the cliff on the northern side of the swimming pool and tore off the outside wall of the power house snapping huge steel girders and leaving others in a twisted tangle. The water pipe leading to the turbine collapsed under the terrific pressure.'

As quickly as it had come, the flood waters dropped. And the sun came out.

Within the short space of 40 minutes, José's dream of a Spanish Castle and Pleasure Grounds had been turned into a scene of total devastation.

Mud, debris, dying plants and trees lay everywhere. All the garden soil had gone; and the tropical orchids that Margarita so treasured. Only the bare rock remained. Paths had been washed away. Huge cedar logs lay stranded throughout the park.

And the buildings were a scene of chaos.

José stood in tears.

There was nothing to say.

Later that evening, tables and chairs from Paronella Park were seen floating downstream towards Innisfail like toy furniture.

Nature had made a mockery of one man's attempt to build a dream in a tropical rainforest.

Chapter Twenty

The next morning the Paronella family surveyed the damage.

José could hardly bear to look at the destruction. He kept shaking his head and saying over and over:

"I never would have thought it could happen. Never. Never."

Margarita recovered quickly. Her practical nature began to assess the situation.

"We're going to need help to clear the debris and mud. We'd better organise that first and then see what can be done to move the cedar logs."

José nodded absentmindedly. He was moving as though in a nightmare.

He followed Margarita as she tried to walk through the upper gardens. Mud was up to her ankles. Vines and creepers blocked the way. She was anxious to check her fernery.

Then she turned to José, silent tears running down her cheeks. A log lay across the flimsy structure. Her priceless collection of maidenhair ferns was totally destroyed.

It was as though fresh flood waters had broken. José and Margarita clung to each other, seeking comfort in their desolation.

Teresa stood to one side, watching her parents. She could not comprehend the impact and significance of the damage. She only knew that never before had she seen her parents sobbing.

There was nothing that she could do.

Fortunately for the Paronella family, they had many friends among the local community. Support came quickly.

Over the next few days, José's friends looked with him at the Park's situation and helped him reach some decisions.

The café by the pool would have to be abandoned. It was irreparable. They would have to concentrate on clearing the Hall and repairing the damage made by the logs. There were huge holes in the walls and the once beautiful parquetry floor was buckled and twisted like a jigsaw.

The upper garden would need clearing and restructuring.

It would mean a change of focus. If the Park were to open again to the public, all food services would have to be moved to the Hall. It would be used less as a cinema and more so as a restaurant and function centre.

The huge cedar logs would have to be cut out from the café and hauled away. This would mean making an access road to the lower park.

Gradually the mammoth task began.

José's first urgent job was to the Hydro Electric plant. This had been put out of action when a tree went through the wall and damaged the system. He looked at it with the help of electrical technicians from the mill.

Their advice was to change the system to A/C. the turbine had originally run at 500rpm. The speed was now increased. José was able to buy a second hand alternator from wartime disposals. This ran at 1500rpm, using a belt system. For electricity for the carbon arc system in the cinema, the A/C would be converted back to D/C,

Work continued on clearing up the rest of the park. But it was costing José a lot of money. And he was not insured against this type of damage. The final cost of the repairs would be in the region of £8000.

It was a period of tremendous financial hardship for the family. Joe was brought home from school. He was needed at home and in any case, they could hardly afford the high boarding and tuition costs. He never went back.

The Park was closed to visitors and consequently, there was no income at all. It would be six months before it reopened for any commercial activity and two years before the ravages of the flood had been completely cleared. The café would never again function. It had become a ruin.

Margarita and Teresa were becoming increasingly concerned about José's health.

Teresa said to her father: "Dad. You're getting so thin."

Finally, Margarita persuaded him to take a break from the Park and all its trauma. They would go to Brisbane. While there, José would consult a specialist, the verdict was quick and absolute.

Cancer of the stomach. Inoperable. Terminal.

Margarita phoned home to tell Teresa.

"Don't let your dad see how upset you are. Get your tears over before we come home."

Teresa recalls that her father still denied that he was ill.

"He would not accept that he had cancer. He tried to carry on as though nothing was wrong. Only, of course, he couldn't. He was vomiting his food up constantly, what little he ate. His strength was slipping away from him."

One morning, José went to the garage to get his car out. He had some business in town. The car wouldn't start, so he climbed out and pushed the car out of the garage, intending to crank start it. The car rolled forward on the slope. José moved to stop it, as he had many times before. But he couldn't. he watched helplessly as the car moved down the hill, heading for the crater drop.

Margarita and Teresa were watching from the cottage window. They assumed José was in the vehicle. Horrified, they saw it bump and lurch towards a certain crash into the 60 foot drop. Miraculously, the wheels stopped, hanging just over the edge. They ran from the house, thinking that car and José would disappear at any moment.

They then saw José standing in front of the garage.

"After that, Mum wasn't too keen on dad driving the car at all. She contacted the local police sergeant and though Joe was too young for a proper licence, they gave him special permission to drive, so that we could still get into town."

José hated to be dependant. He had always been a strong man, a worker. Now he had to rely on others. He took it very badly.

Frequently he was short-tempered and cranky. At other times, he seemed withdrawn inside his own thoughts.

There was so much unresolved.

What would happen to Paronella Park when he died? Would the family be able to carry on? Young Joe's heart didn't seem to be in the business. And Margarita couldn't cope with it on her own. Perhaps she would remarry? She was only 46 years old.

And Teresa? He spoke to her about Aldo.

"He's not going to come back for you. Find a good man, one who wants to stay here and work at the Park."

And yet, he thought, does it really matter? His Park? His dream? It would never be the same again.

And what about Albie - and Jackie?

Who would be there to see they lived a reasonable life? That they didn't drink and get caught up with bad company?

He felt so impotent. It couldn't all be slipping away? So quickly?

It seemed only yesterday that he had stood at the top of Mena Creek Falls and promised himself: 'Here I will build my Castle.'

José's last months were approaching. He soon lost so much strength and was in such great pain that he could not walk around the grounds.

One day, Joe got out the bike José had always loved to ride. He helped him onto the seat.

"It was like lifting a puppet onto the saddle. He was too weak to pedal so I held him on and wheeled him along the paths."

At least José had one last look at his creation.

After this, he was more or less confined to bed. It was a slow, lingering death.

Close to the end, a Spanish boy, the son of friends, came over to the cottage to help Margarita.

José needed to use the bedpan. Young Stanley Onaindia helped him.

"He was just a set of bones. There was no flesh on him at all."

José Paronella, the Spanish dreamer, passed away at 6.30am on 23rd August 1948.

He died in Margarita's arms.

In Innisfail cemetery, a small plaque records José's last resting place.

At Mena Creek still stands the memorial he had always dreamed about - Paronella Park.

The Paronella Family

Written in 1997

The dream comes alive again

The new owners, Judy and Mark Evans, are totally committed to preserving José's Paronella Park and reviving his dream.

They bring new energy and fresh ideas to give Paronella Park a renewed vitality. Under their guidance, the Park is once again becoming a major tourist attraction. Their first task has been to improve the appearance of the grounds with major garden reconstructions.

Judy and Mark want to encourage people to use the Park in increasing numbers - to bring a picnic and relax by the water; to cool off in the pool or stroll through the grounds. Visitors can once again enjoy wonderful Paronella afternoon teas, sitting in Margarita's cottage, which is now a café.

And the Park is once again becoming popular for weddings. The ceremony is held in the romantic setting of the lawns in front of the café ruins. Afterwards, guests can enjoy a reception in the upper gardens, overlooking the Falls.

But this is only the beginning of plans for the renewal of the enterprise. There is a ten year plan, designed to bring to fruition Judy and Mark's own dreams.

"We have already built a museum dedicated to José Paronella. This will house documents and photos of the Paronella family and the early years of the Park. Many local people have donated china, souvenirs and postcards."

Mark continued: "The museum is only one way of preserving José's achievements for future generations. We have future plans to bring the Hydro Electric plant back into use. This will be a very costly enterprise, but as well as showing José's scheme functioning, it will enable us to illuminate the whole park at night, with floodlighting for the castle tower and lights slung above the paths and bridges."

The next major development will be to build a hall, a replica of José's ballroom. It will be like walking back into history. There will be the parquetry floor, the red and blue velvet drapes, and the revolving ball."

So if you come to Paronella Park in the future, you may be able to dance the night away in José's ballroom under the coloured lights. Then perhaps, a quiet moment on the terrace or a romantic stroll through the grounds.

It may not be possible to restore the crumbling ruins of José's buildings. But Judy and Mark may be in time to preserve the magic of his vision; the inspiration of a man of optimism and idealism - the Spanish Dreamer, José Paronella.

2009

The Dream Continues ...

This year has seen the completion of the refurbishment of the original Hydro Electric System (installed 1933).

The next project is to create an Interpretation Centre which will be extensively used by schools and special interest groups.

With current technology and the park's growing popularity we will begin work on stabilising the park's structures.

2010, the 75th anniversary of the opening of the Park, will see a new tourism venture being launched in Cairns. A dining /theatre experience presenting José Paronella's story will be launched in Cairns, titled "The Impossible Dream".

This will ensure the story of Paronella Park lives on.

Original Hydro Electric System Refurbished, November 2009

Map as shown in guide book used in the 1950's

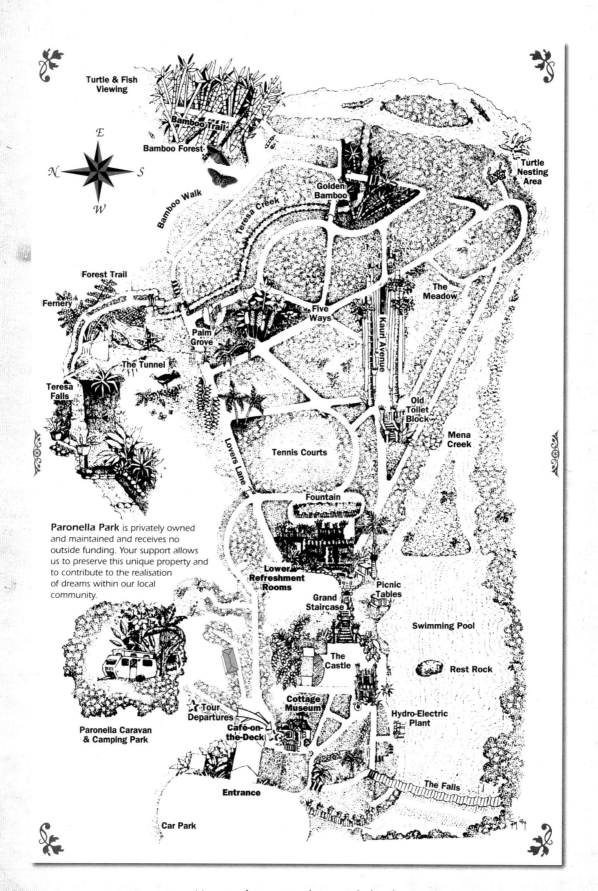

Map as shown in todays guide book

The Park Entrance as it was in 1993

The Park Entrance today, 2010

Paronella Park

Diving platform by the falls

Crowds enjoying a swim in 1934

Walk to the Tunnel of Love

"Paronella Park ... The Dream Continues" TV Promotion, 2001